THE
POOR
SAVE US

MEGAN McKENNA

Published by:

Clear Faith Publishing, LLC
718 Caxambas Drive
Marco Island, FL 34145
www.clearfaithpublishing.com

Cover and interior design by Doug Cordes

The interior is typeset in Brocha and Blacker

ISBN: 978-1-940414-28-7

Cover Photo: Fr. Les Paquin

The mission of Clear Faith Publishing is to spread joy, peace, and comfort through
great writing about spirituality, religion, and faith that touches the reader and
serves those who live on the margins. Portions of the proceeds from our Hom-
ilists for the Homeless series are donated to organizations that feed, shelter, and
provide counsel for those in need. For more information, please visit us at www.
clearfaithpublishing.com.

Dedication

With Les and all the poor ones, the friends of the Son of Man whose stories have not yet been told, but who are saving us even now. With gratitude for how you bless our lives.

Contents

Contents *(continued)*

Introduction

We are all familiar with the mission statement of Jesus, words spoken in the synagogue at the beginning of his public ministry:

"The spirit of the Lord has been given to me for he has annointed me to bring good news to the poor, to proclaim liberty to captives, and to the blind new sight, to set the downtrodden free, to proclaim the Lord's Year of favour." (Luke 4:18 – 19).

While studying for the priesthood I found it easy to reflect on this call as we had a mission in the poorer region of northeastern Brazil. I would be given the great privilege of working amongst the poor for 9 years. I would discover much about our mission and relationship to the poor.

With the dawn of liberation theology the Latin American church held several ecumenical councils such as Puebla, Medellín and São Domingos. The church started talking about the preferential option for the poor.

It was more than a choice among many alternatives; it is an imperative without which the church fails to be church. We are called to walk in solidarity with the poor. They will show us the way to salvation. We need them. We cannot be fully alive without them. The poor always have something to give. In journeying with the poor, the hungry, the thirsty, the stranger, the prisoner we discover the face of Jesus himself. They are also like a mirror in which we discover our own neediness and poverties.

Who is the little girl on the cover of the book? In general terms she represents the poor. In specific terms she is the little Marias we are called to love. In reality Maria has a very difficult life. Her father is an unemployed sugar cane cutter. With no welfare or unemployment insurance they are living a hand to mouth existence. They joined other families that compose Brazil's land reform movement. They are squatting on land that is not being cultivated. They live in tents made of plastic and cardboard. Water from a small stream is used for bathing, washing and drinking. Parasites abound. Chickens run about. The landless are persecuted by the land owner's hired guns.

Churches bring bags of rice and beans, notebooks and first aid supplies. Highways are blocked in protest by the landless to speed up land appropriations. Often it takes up to 15 years of struggle and hardship to get title to the land. What a celebration of faith every time we visit the landless. What a celebration when the poor find the Promised Land.

Maria is beautiful, playful, innocent, The landless poor showed me and gave me many things; gratitude, hospitality, community, courage, hope, faithfulness and joy. Riches I still carry with even today.

In many ways the poor as described gave and taught me a lot about my own poverty. The poor always have something to give. Though our diocesan church proclaimed the good news to the poor, it is the poor who have given so much to our church. We need them more than they needed us.

I gave a copy of Maria's picture to Megan McKenna after a retreat she preached at St.Philip Neri parish in my home diocese in Canada. She keeps it on her as a reminder that she is to walk in solidarity with God's poor. I challenged her to write a book of stories of how God has touched her through God's poor. A daunting task but done with love and gratitude. Thank you for reminding us to walk with the poor. There is no salvation without them! Thank you Megan!

FR. LES PAQUIN

This is the book that was written at the urging of my missionary friend (not my usual reason for writing a book). And it was written differently than all the others—in long hand in a notebook that I carried around with me as I travelled over two-three years (interrupted by a hiatus to have quadruple bypass surgery). The request was to write a book about my faith and struggles; how the scriptures impact my living of the Good News to the Poor and how the poor taught me and revealed to me my own poverty, simply put, how the poor save me. It had to be about people. They were the source of the insights and belief—that I knew right away but finding a way to share these people that I have been privileged and honored to meet wasn't as easy to share. They were buried deep inside me like seeds that had grown and flowered and now were to be uprooted, cut or transplanted to be shared.

Two things or two stories have served as both the catalyst as to who was remembered and why they had such an impact on me. The first story is connected to a Latin American theologian Jon Sobrino. He has written a good number of books, one of his more recent, but less known ones is entitled THE EYE OF THE NEEDLE: No Salvation Outside the Poor: A Utopian-Prophetic Essay (translated by Dinah Livingsgtone, Darton, Longman and Todd, Londonm, 2008.) The book is short with only 96 pages including footnotes, etc., but it is dense, evocative and provocative. And the book reminds me of an experience and story that I cannot forget.

Jon Sobrino is forever bound to his friends: the six Jesuits he lived and worked with and their housekeeper and her daughter in El Salvador. He was away lecturing in Southeast Asia when a military hit squad entered the university grounds and butchered them all—looking specifically for Ignacio Ellacuria, his closest friend and Jon himself. They were all murdered, with the killers assuming they have gotten him as well. When Jon heard the news he was devastated. Eight people he loved were dead and he was one of the intended victims. He disappeared for a number of years, retreating, going to counseling, seeking healing, working and writing in seclusion until he returned to El Salvador, where the people he served and loved gave him back life and hope. Their faith and vitality, their forgiveness and hope in dealing with the hate and violence they too had endured gave him life again.

Eventually he was invited to speak at a university in the States and accepted. Throughout the trip and upon arrival, people would ask him: How are you? (incessantly) and he'd answer: I'm fine, thank you. It was awkward. Finally, he stood to speak and thanked people for the invitation and their concern. He began by saying: I know you all want to know how I am. I am fine. He paused and then continued. You see, I'm a friend of the Son of Man. There was not a sound in the room. No one moved. Then looking at all the blank faces, he went on: Oh, you don't know what I mean—let me introduce you to the Son of Man. He spoke.

Imagine that you die today and as you approach the gates of heaven you are shocked to see that Jesus, the Crucified and Risen One stands before you, clothed in white, shining like the sun, with the marks of his passion on him, but cloaked in glory. The two of you stand facing one another. Nothing is said though you know you are being seen and judged. As you stand looking at him (you can't not look, as you are seen into so deeply) you begin to realize there are a number of people standing right behind him.

Your gaze is drawn to them and one by one you look at them and it takes a moment to admit that you know them. Each person is someone you harmed or treated unjustly or violently in your life. And you see the effect of your actions or inaction on them from that moment forward. And you see Jesus just looking at you. And you unknowingly take a step back from the Son of Man.

But his gaze is steadfast and you must continue to be seen and to see. And then you see that there are more people behind the first group. One by one they arise in your memory and how they entered your life. You realize that each of these people is someone you could have helped, responded to or accompanied for awhile, but you did not. And again you are witness to the effects your choices had on their lives, for evil or for good. And again you take another step away from the Son of Man.

Jesus, the Son of Man is still looking at you and there is no escape from his eyes on your heart and soul and there are now more and more people behind him. You are drawn to them yet again. It seems they go on forever. And you begin to realize how each one of these people were touched for better or worse by your decisions and your collusion with evil. They are bound to every group you were connected to and a part of: your nation and country; your economic and political systems, your educational institutions, recreational groups; and church and religious affiliations, your friends and family. It begins to dawn on you that we are all one, more bound to one another than you ever imagined before. And again you step back from the Son of Man.

Finally, Jesus looks away from you and turns his back on you, facing all those other people and says, very firmly and clearly: "What do you say, do we let him/her in?"

He paused (his back now to the audience) and turned again to face everyone, saying: Now you know the Son of Man. I am fine. I am good. I am friends with the Son of Man. And then he gave his talk.

I did not know him, not really. I had met him once or twice in Latin America—usually at breakfast in a house or community where I was staying, over toast, pan dulce, eggs, and coffee, before each of us went our ways for the day. After the talk when I found myself beside him in a group, we spoke for a moment. He remembered my face and connected me to some of the missionaries I had worked with. I awkwardly repeated his words: You are friends with the Son of Man? He started to smile and nodded. Without thinking I said: are we friends? He smiled more broadly and put his hand on my arm, saying Yes—and if you have trouble being friends with the Son of Man, make friends with a friend of the Son of Man. We were interrupted and he was drawn off into another conversation.

I was nailed to the floor and couldn't respond. His reply has echoed and reverberated inside me, persistent like a mantra, a command, ever since. I must be friends with the Son of Man and when that seems impossible or unlikely, then I must make friends with a friend of the Son of Man.

The other story that situates all these accounts of wisdom shared and life given more abundantly to me was told to me in Japan many years ago. I was visiting a monastery and a stranger welcomed me, and pointed out an older woman in hushed tones. Everyone I met spoke about her, usually saying: That's her. And I would respond Who? And I was told the story.

A young woman Jiya-Kennett was training at Sojiji Temple in Japan in the early 1960s. She was surprised one day by the arrival of an important visitor. She had just come back from a day in the city and as she entered the temple gardens there was a contingent of priests and women in the abbot's guest area and in the center of the gathering there was a middle-aged woman who looked kind, and at ease being the focus of attention. The woman smiled at her as she arrived but no one offered introductions so she went up to the woman, smiled back and held out her hand. The other woman shook her hand with obvious delight, even a bit of laughter, enjoying meeting her and held her hand for a few moments. It took a moment or two but Jiya-Kennett thought that everyone seemed startled and some stared, but nobody said anything. The older woman replied to her in English, telling the young woman that she was glad that she was studying there and that she hoped that she'd see her again on her next visit.

Soon after Jiya went back to her rooms since she really didn't know any of the other guests or dignitaries. She settled in to have tea and the director of the temple in charge of long term guests came to her door. He stood in the doorway and said: I want you to shake hands with me. She bowed to him, and politely asked why. His answer shocked her. You shook the hand of the empress of Japan. No living person has touched that hand other than the emperor. You do not realize what a great thing you have done! She didn't know what to say, or how to react, but solemnly shook his hand.

A few moments later her door was knocked on again and this time the whole staff of the monastery from the gardeners, to maintenance people and cooks, and every other student, monk and even the abbot were lined up, with their hands extended, even the junior monks were lined up in neat rows. Every one of them wanted her to shake hands with them, and did. Jiju-Kennett wrote later 'that shaking the hand of...her who shook the hand is the next best thing to shaking the hand!'

And I learned over the years that making friends with the friends of the Son of Man was the next best thing to being friends with the Son of Man. And the poor are the privileged place of revelation as well as the preferred place where the Son of Man, our God hides out.

To touch the hand or to be a friend of the poor is to touch the hand and be the friend of the Son of Man. And hanging out, visiting with them and being befriended by the poor makes it possible to stand before the Son of Man, let him look at us and look back—the first gesture of being friends with Jesus, the Son of Man.

These stories are some of my moments when I touched the hand of the Son of Man in touching the hand of one of his friends, a poor one. I've been blessed again and again by these people touching me and impacting my soul and heart until forever. When I have difficulty being friends with the Son of Man, crucified, risen and come in glory to judge the earth and its nations and all peoples with justice—then I am befriended by someone (who is poor and beloved of God) and I am bound together with them as friends until forever. I am saved again and again. In gratitude I share these stories, a small way perhaps of you touching the hand of one who holds the hand of the Son of Man and a nudge to remember his friends who visit your life. We are all one more than we could ever imagine, but will know one day. Peace be with you.

MEGAN McKENNA

Preface

I MET MEGAN MCKENNA in Detroit about ten years ago at a session where we both were teaching Scripture. I will not forget the sensation of sitting in on her first lecture. I was mesmerized as she spoke, quoting the Scripture from memory and interpreting it without stammering or stuttering, with a powerful and clear focus. A few hours later, she sat in on my presentation. As I read through my copious notes and glanced up only occasionally at the audience, I saw her looking at me. When I finished, she walked up to me and said directly and clearly: "Good content, bad delivery! Throw away those notes." I was taken aback at first by her boldness in speaking so brutally to someone she had just met. However, I immediately perceived the truth in her comment and that inspired me to an act of faith that transformed my teaching: I threw away the notes and have never looked back.

It was in that encounter with Megan that I discovered the vast difference between teaching, commenting on, analyzing, and preaching the Gospel. Megan is a preacher of Good News. She herself bears witness to this in her story "Wisdom Plays before the Lord" when she writes, "I knew that I was called to preach the gospel, in season and out and to proclaim the Scriptures, telling them with my heart, looking at people and summoning them to hear, face to face—whenever, wherever I could." Proclaiming means looking at people, looking through their eyes into their souls and laying bare what is there. The stories in this volume do just that!

Over the years, as I liberated myself more and more from written texts and notes, I discovered what Megan had sought to teach. The Gospel is preached not only with one's voice and mind but with one's whole being. One is called to be fully alive, right in the face of those hearing the Word so that the Word might be received as fully alive. The proclaimer of Good News is not simply interpreting the words of Scripture but is witnessing to the life of the Word contained in the Scripture. In her essay "Discernment", Megan writes, "Religion is perhaps this: to make the stories of God come true today in us, as Jesus the Word made Flesh dwelling among us continues the Good News to the poor in our flesh and histories together."

Seeing Megan in action, with her fiery and contagious passion, one can sense a real succession from the earliest proclaimers of the Gospel to those who bring the Word alive today. Through the generations, a moment of profound conversion inevitably involves hearing. Paradigmatically, sinful King David was awoken from his unconscious by hearing the parable of the prophet Nathan. Drawn into the story of the poor man, whose beloved lamb was robbed by the callous rich man, David proclaimed judgment and Nathan exclaimed, *"You are the man!"* (2 Samuel 12:7). David's greatness is revealed even here in this moment of profound sin; he can hear.... Hearing leads him on a road to contrition and conversion, to reconciliation and restoration.

However, we are in dire need of those who make the Word audible. Saint Paul, in his Letter to the Romans, writes: *"For, 'Everyone who calls on the name of the Lord shall be saved.' But how are they to call on one in whom they have not believed? And how are they to believe in one of whom they have never heard? And how are they to hear without someone to proclaim him? And how are they to proclaim him unless they are sent? As it is written, 'How beautiful are the feet of those who bring good news!'"* (Romans 10:13–15). Perhaps more than ever, we need those willing to call out, as *"a voice crying out in the wilderness"* (Mark 1:3, inspired by Isaiah 40:3). That voice is too often alone, going against the current, yet radiant with faith and joyful in the knowledge that this is a vocation and a mission.

The one called to proclaim Good News is the one who knows how to listen. Listening to God in moments of deep prayer and silence is one aspect. Megan describes these moments of prayer in her essay, "Beijing Prayer" as: *"Mostly, I just try to stop, to be quiet, sit or stand still before God and let God look at me."* However, listening is not only an intensely intentional act directed toward

God but also a focused and loving act directed toward humanity and a world in the throes of war and disorder, suffering and pain.... Listening intently to humanity not only enables one to clearly see the darkness but also to identify the light, the goodness, and the resilience.

Megan McKenna is a preacher of Good News. We need to hear her, be filled with the Word she proclaims, and set off as she has, following Him who leads us on and calls us to be His companions and collaborators. With her, we want to deepen our faith that "*God is great. God is good. God lives in this neighborhood.*"

REV. DAVID M. NEUHAUS, SJ
JERUSALEM

God's Eyes

THE SMALL GIRL CHILD (on the cover) is Maria and she's five years old in the photograph, from a barrio in Brazil. Her face in the black-and-white photo was a small gift from a friend who spent years as a missionary in her world. She's been on my wall now for more than twelve years, looking out at me, when I write, prepare classes and presentations, and sometimes, pray the Spirit to rush upon me with insight and inscape. She stands there, vulnerable, wide open, watching intently, leaning up against the thin tree trunk. We've become old friends.

She always stops my mind's running around and draws me into her world. The invitation is almost impossible to deny or resist. I always begin to smile as she questions me: Who are you? It is posed with clarity and innocence (though it is also apparent that her life has been hard physically). She is one of the poor ones. She asks: Do you see me?

Over the years my answer has changed often. It took me a long while to realize (I miss the obvious sometimes) that what I see—her face, her eyes looking at me, seeing me—are the eyes of God, the eyes of the poor, beckoning me to draw near, come close, be friends. (I've been told by a Jewish friend and scholar that "to pray" means to stand in the presence of God and be seen (truth be told), stay and not turn or run away. It also means to contemplate, in Thomas Merton's words: a long, loving look at reality. I add on—reality that is painful and hard to look at and absorb, until it touches heart and soul. So much of reality is tinged with sorrow, lack, sadness, grief, poverty, injustice, even death—especially when it comes all too soon, too often violently, at the extremes of life—being born, letting go and at the last, dying into forever.

She is all that, the eyes of a child, the eyes of the poor, the eyes of God forthrightly gazing back at me (at all of us). The photo has become an icon, mirroring truths that cannot easily be put into words, that both repel and reveal, put off, startle, and draw us in magnetically—beyond. In the shadows there is such delight, wide openness, irresistible joy, keenness, and asking: Do you see what I see? Who are you? Who are we?

Many Indigenous Peoples (First Nations) still know that eyes are the windows to the soul and so are often reluctant to look you right in the eye. Their eyes move down toward the ground or away to the sky. To look you in the eye in public is often considered rude, aggressive, even accosting. It is done on certain occasions: in ritual, enclosed in sacred time and space, with an elder or family member, in moments of transition—when they feel guarded by tradition. This gaze is saved for moments of shared intimacy and privacy. It is worth noting that when we look at someone's eyes closely, what we see is our own face and image clearly, near perfectly reflected back toward us.

I remember with shock the first time I saw this happening before my eyes (I had been warned ahead of time by an elder on some things to do and not do when I was storytelling in the communities). I heard and watched a teacher in the class where I was visiting. She was shouting at one of the young children:" Look at me when I'm talking to you. What are you afraid of? What did you do that you don't want me to know about?" The poor fourth grade child was torn and in distress. All he had ever known and been taught was that he must be respectful and cast his eyes down, and listen with care and attentiveness. Now he was being publicly chastised and humiliated and worse, told to disobey his heritage and foundational principles. He finally did look up. What I saw was pain too deep for so young a spirit to understand, and guilt. It was a terrible sight.

I was told a long time ago by an elderly Orthodox Jew that prayer is being seen by God, the Holy One, blessed be His Name, letting God look at you and looking back at God, facing the truth of what God sees in us, and remaining there—like Moses before the burning bush that was on fire, yet was not consumed—being fiercely seared and burned, but alive. It echoed the more formal definition given to me earlier. These are terrifying moments when we become burning bushes for one another!

And sometimes these moments are rare blessings. We are given that sight of God and what God sees in us, when we are seen in the eyes of another. It can be a shock to one's soul! And a rush of pure delight! It is light that penetrates cold bones and still hearts, laying one bare—utterly vulnerable, when suddenly all our guards are gone, laid down, and we are given a glimpse of pure truth. And in that flash of a second's recognition we are held dear with such freshness—reflected in God's eyes, touched by God's lingering gaze. And we know we have been set free, liberated so we can exist and live full of grace and truth.

This book is a litany made of such blessings, and prayed on paper so they can be shared. All the stories tell of being caught off guard by God's eyes looking straight at me, through me, through the eyes of people I met. Their presence, their being there with me, was sheer gift that has remained and dwelled in me ever since. They are moments when God visited his people. They were and still are pure, raw invitations and public intimacies—doors and windows thrown open as the light poured in through them, in the twinkling of an eye. They are glances of God grazing into my soul; and like glass breaking, my heart was broken open and shattered. They became shards that I carry as they keep opening my soul and eyes to a bit of how God sees us.

Each is a moment when I was taken from blindness to sight, a beginning that told me, demanded that I stay, see and be seen, and have my world shattered into rainbows, prisms of truth. Each time was God winking at me, undoing me and revealing, playfully and devastatingly, that God is transfiguring all of reality, all the time. This is transfiguration: seeing through and into the mystery of the Trinity, passing through them and in their eyes, God's eyes, being drawn into communion, becoming one as our God is. I have never forgotten and have never recovered from these transfigurations and am forever grateful to have been saved again and again by these marvelous children of God whom I share this world with, along with God's risen presence among us.

Probably many of the people in these encounters would be described as poor, those people blessed by God as already having the kingdom, the communion of God within them, among them. They each and all gave their greatest treasure graciously (often unknowingly) to a stranger, a visitor, an outsider. Their flesh and blood, bones and eyes held the Word of God made visible. Each one has saved me. I tell their stories in hopes that their wisdom and their loveliness will save you too. This is the proclamation, the preaching of the Good News to the poor, who are always the privileged place of revelation and the place to meet the presence of God most strongly.

It is said in the earlier Testament that if you see God, you die. In the more recent testament it remains the same: see God, die, and then rise to see him again. Every time we see God in one another, anywhere, under any guise, we are caught in the net, thrown out by others—the way our God catches us now. And once caught, may others look at us and see such glory, such goodness, such a glimmer of God looking back at them through our eyes.

Beijing Prayer

I T WAS MY FIRST visit, over a decade or more ago—around 2002. I was there a couple of weeks. Saw all the usual tourist places and sights, though I was staying in a house in Tianjin (fourth largest city in the country) about an hour by car from Beijing. Saw the Great Wall, even climbed up to the broken pieces scattered along a ridge—in a segment that had not been restored—rough climb but it gave a better sense of its immensity and what a project it was, stretching for miles across the country. And was in Tiananmen Square, seeing the great palaces, gardens, and old buildings from the turn-of-the-century past—built in the 1880s through 1930s— even the Peking Opera and small villages between the two cities where I was the first white woman most of the children had ever seen, and the poverty was abysmal—like walking back a hundred years.

Finally, I had just a few days to wander around by myself. I chose the older area of the city, with markets, shops and small places to eat, parks to sit and watch people. Inevitably they would come and want their pictures taken with the foreigner and try out a few words of English. The school children were usually the first to approach; then the elders, smiling and bowing. Then I wandered into shops— the usual tourist things: lanterns, fans, old books and some antiques, and high-end art galleries. I love everything old—the pottery, painted porcelain, raiku, earthen vessels, copper stands and plates, incense burners and intricately designed tea sets.

I stopped into one. Everything was outrageously expensive, way beyond anything I could afford. But I was enjoying the gorgeous array of ancient plates, huge bowls, urns and vases, the delicate statues. I moved carefully around to look at pieces, careful not to be "a bull in a China shop!"

A young woman came over to me. She was about twenty-three or twenty-four, and she was excited, wanting to practice her English with me—which was far better than my handful of Chinese phrases that I'd picked up. We bowed to each other, smiling. She wanted to show me pieces (hoping I'd buy) so I told her I didn't have money but was just enjoying all the exquisite treasures. We exchanged pleasantries: where I was from: born in New York, living in New Mexico—a bit of geography on a piece of paper, makeshift map. That it was my first time in China, and I had been in Tianjin and a portion of the Wall not open to the public. Then where she was from: more than fifty hours by train from Beijing, further west, toward mountains! She was excited to tell me that she was learning English—online! Since no one was in the shop, she asked, changing her tone of voice, "May we speak?"

I said, "Of course."

Her next question was, "Are you a Christian?"

I answered, "Yes, a Catholic."

There was a very pregnant moment of silence. Then she asked me if I prayed. Surprised, I almost stuttered and said, "Yes, I do."

Her answer surprised me again. She said, "I thought so. You have white hair." She had earlier asked me how old I was, and with hand gestures (using my fingers/and the palm of my hand) I told her I was fifty-seven (though my hair had been white since I was in my late twenties). She told me (as others had already) that in Taoism, white hair, especially on one so young, meant that I'd been touched by the Spirits, the gods, and had great power. I didn't say anything—what could I say?

She was very serious and said she'd found a lot of information on a website that said Christians prayed to their gods: to change the weather and make it suit an occasion; for money; for a job; for getting a visa to travel to another country; to make someone who was sick, better, and to keep people from dying. I listened and said, "Yes. Some people do that but those ways of praying aren't the only ways."

"Oh," she said, "like the Tao."

"Yes! You can pray in thanksgiving or when you are aware of the beauty of the earth, sky, waters, and all that exists around you that was made by the Creator. Or you can pray for people and what they might need as they try to live a balanced life—and you can pray for yourself, to be a better person—or you can just talk things over with God.

Again, there was a pause heavy with quiet. Then she asked me how was the best way to pray—a strong way—how did I pray? I nearly panicked; what could I say with our limited grasp of a common language? I said a fast, fervent prayer to the Spirit to give me wisdom and words—simple that would be good for her to know, and I started.

"Mostly, I just try to stop, to be quiet, to sit or stand still before God and let God look at me. And I try to look back and talk without words and listen to whatever might be said. I remember that God made me and that he loves me and wants me to live as he did—imitating Jesus who cared for everyone, especially those in need, the poor and the infirm and the hungry, and that we must be just with each other."

She listened intently and then looked around. There was no one else in the shop, and she asked, "Can you tell me exactly how to do it? Teach me and then I'll go in the back room for about ten to fifteen minutes and try and see if I can do it."

Uh, duh. I took a deep breath and said, "Sit or stand, whatever is comfortable for you. Be very still. Close your eyes if it helps. Listen to your heart. You are alive and God keeps you alive, and it's God's spirit that breathes in you. Be still and just be with God and let God look at you. Remember He loves you and wants you to live and be like God, live in peace and be what you were born to be (what your face was like before you were born; she understood that from her tradition), and be true. (She had read/heard a little about Jesus and knew that he showed us how to live.) Then I ended with: "Don't ask for anything. Just be there and try to stay very attentive."

She nodded and asked me to stay in the shop and if anyone came in to tell them that she'd be back in about ten to fifteen minutes. I nodded: "Of course; I'll be happy to." And off she went to the small back room, the supply/stock area. I prayed that I had said the right words and she would have all she needed—and that God would do the rest.

After about fifteen minutes she reappeared, smiling and bowing and thanking me with folded hands; bowing again and again, *xie xie* (which means Thank You—it sounds like shay shay when spoken).

We looked at each other and then she said, "I sat quiet and let God be with me. I know now: God made me. God is with me. God is good. God is power. God is truthful; he takes care of me, all of us. God wants me to be free and be a good human being and he will stay with me. There is nothing to be afraid of; no one to fear. No one owns me. I am free. And I can be at peace and bring peace to the world. God will help me do what is good."

I was stunned. She got all that in less than fifteen minutes? At first go? My God, I thought—she prayed. And I don't think I have ever prayed in my life! We hugged and held each other. I took her picture and asked her what her name was in Chinese: "Autumn Graces," and I told her mine. She asked, "Will you remember me?"

"Oh yes! I will remember you and pray for you every day—and you must pray for me." We smiled—a lot! And bowed—a lot! And someone entered the shop, setting the chimes ringing. I moved across the room toward the door, and we both smiled and bowed gently, deeply for the last time. And I left.

I have never, ever forgotten her for a moment. I even went back the next afternoon to see if she was there still, but it was someone else minding the shop. I went back that night to my borrowed bedroom and sat on the floor and tried to pray—as a novice, starting over as though it were the first time, deeply humbled, knowing how much I had to learn and acutely aware that I knew very little, if anything about praying and being still before God—just sitting there and letting God look at me and looking back, listening and becoming more what God has dreamed that I become as a human being. That young woman, "Autumn Graces" (I was in China in October), was the gift China gave to me.

Feet, Shoes, and Shortening the Way

I T WAS MY FIRST (and only) visit to South Africa, and I was overwhelmed with the vastness of the land, the continent. If I traveled east or west to get to the country from my home in New Mexico, it was a three-day journey flying. There were great distances to cover in going from one place to the next: towns, villages off the main highways, then secondary roads and, finally, dirt roadways. There were all manners of transportation—buses, vans, cars, motor bikes, bicycles, and so many walking along on the sides of the roads. So many on their way to work, to get daily food and water, and to go to school or visit relatives.

One of the first things I noticed was that most of the children heading out in the morning for school were barefoot, in uniforms, carrying their side packs. When I arrived at a school just as they were gathering to sing the beginning of the day, I was shocked to see them brushing off their feet with their fingers, scraping off the caked mud, dust, and bits of trash and garbage picked up along the way, and then carefully drawing their shoes out of their packs and putting them on to wear while in school. I was told by my "minder," who had invited me to his schools for six weeks, that this way the shoes will last longer. Even when their feet outgrow the shoes, they can pass them on to others in the family. I was traveling for six weeks just in this country of South Africa, and I had three pairs of shoes with me. They were sandals, hiking boots, and a pair to wear whenever I was in someone's house or teaching in public places. (I went home with just the sandals on my feet.)

When I'd teach all day in workshops, we'd start around ten in the morning and go to four p.m. Most of those attending came from villages many miles away and walked for two, three, or even four hours to get to the meeting place. They brought food to supplement what they would have as a snack break and lunch—and when we were finished, they would set out once more for the trip home. They told me the trip home was harder, being tired, but they enjoyed it more because they'd retell the stories and the Scriptures that I had told them during the day and then add in their own stories and experiences, continuing what we'd started earlier. They would smile broadly and say it made the way shorter.

I found myself, whenever I'd be invited to eat with them, asking them for their stories. I had maybe a dozen to tell, gleaned and discovered through research and others telling me them in the States and from many countries in Africa, and I was hungry for more—for their stories. I'd listen and then when I was back wherever I was staying that night, I'd try to remember and write them down as best I could. I stayed awhile in Soweto in one of the larger townships at the invitation of the women who organized the blocks in groups. They'd read the Scriptures weekly and talk about them. Then they'd talk about their neighbors in the block and try to make sure that everyone had some food. Often the lights would go out—you had to feed the one electrical outlet with coins (and the stove) for the next half hour. Sometimes we just stayed in the dark, getting used to the shadows, and continued talking, listening closely to one another. Usually there was only one small window in the concrete blocks, with a sheet or a piece of cloth draped from the ceiling to separate sections of the one room, so there wasn't much light even during the day. I learned that listening and hearing the other voices in the dark heightened the meaning and intent of words, adding a dimension of knowledge and experience that could be heard—another language.

Everywhere I went, each area of South Africa was like another country and I was always asked what did I want to see, where did I want to go. I wanted to go to Robeson Island where Nelson Mandela had been imprisoned (and I did go to the museum where he'd been jailed earlier). I told them I wanted to see some of the animals. They told me I had to see the big five, especially after I told a story about coming of age in the community by seeing and looking into the eyes of a lion, a rhino, a snake, and an elephant, and letting them look back. They added in zebras, hippos, water buffaloes, crocodiles, and giraffes. I saw all of them, though I only saw the lions through my telephoto lens, at a safe distance. But I said that the one thing I really wanted to do was to travel to the very end of the continent and go in the water. I had read that there was a place where you could stand in the water where the two oceans—the Indian and the South Atlantic—came together, with two different kinds of tides and where even the temperature of the waters was noticeably different, and the salt content. It was the mixing and blending place, liminal where two worlds of water came together. There were many nodding heads when I said that. I got to the Horn and looked out over the edge of the land, but the waters were incredibly rough after strong storms and it was rocky and windy—far too dangerous to try to even wade in the water. The actual beach that I had read about was still miles further south, so I never did get to experience that coming together.

At a closing meal in my honor, women from each tribe or group that I had worked with came up and sang and danced, drummed one of their traditional songs (in their distinctive long pieces-of-cloth skirts and hats that matched). And then they told me one of their stories, often acting out the parts of the animals, the moon and sun, stars, rain, plants, and winds. I was entranced but despaired of ever remembering all of them. They all started to blur and merge together in my mind. But at the end of the feasting I was given a gift. I was presented with a cloth book! Each group of women had made a page or two, sewing the words of a story and recipes for something I had eaten onto the cloth pages—often with illustrations to describe and flesh out the imagery—so that I could take their stories and words with me. I told them it was a grand gift. When I was very young, the first book I could remember was a cloth book made by my nana that I had treasured but lost along the way. This one would more than take its place among my treasures.

The six weeks were overwhelming. They kept saying, "You must come back." Encountering and experiencing just the country of South Africa in my mid-sixties told me that I would need another sixty years to even begin to get a feel for them, to delve into the richness and diversity of their cultures and wisdom, or just to see their lands. I haven't been back since (sigh).

The day I was to leave, I was staying overnight in a B and B in Johannesburg before going to the airport on the first leg home, to Germany. About an hour before we left, there was a knock at the front door and I was told that I had a visitor. I couldn't imagine who it might be. I came down, and in the hall was a tall, thin young man in his early twenties. I didn't recognize him. He was all smiles and had a brown paper bag that he couldn't wait to give me. He blurted out that he was so afraid that he'd be too late and miss me. He had heard the stories and talk from his aunties who had been at the very first all-day workshop I'd done weeks ago. "They told me you wanted to go into the waters where the oceans come together but never got there. I used to live near there and it's a place full of power, fear, and wonder. It tells you how small you are and how great you are too. I was sorry that you didn't get there."

I was touched by his concern. Then he handed me the paper bag. "This is for you—it comes from there—in the waters." I opened the bag to find a perfect moon shell, shining softly, ecru, white, pink streaked, smooth as alabaster, larger than his hand—which was twice the size of mine. I was speechless. It was such an exquisite thing. Right away he wanted to know if I could take it back home with me, saying that it was made by the ocean floor being rubbed by the waters and that some creature left it behind as it made its way along the beach. I nodded and started crying. I didn't know what to say.

I blurted out the question: "You got this for me?" His great smile reappeared and I stuttered on: "It's so far away (we'd gone by car toward where the land ends. It was a good day's journey).

He said simply, "Yes, I know the way. It was home for me for a long time. I walked."

I just stood there, mute. He continued. "The old ones say: anything you do and wherever you go, the journey isn't that long when it's on your way home." What could I say? His gift of the shell, his words, his walking, his time and expenditure of energy and care! I just wrapped my arms around him. When we let go he said, "It's not just from me. It's from my aunties and family, too, so you can take us home with you." I will always remember. The moon in the water; the moon in the night sky; the moon curved over us all. We are all walking home together. We are all gift to one another.

Israel and
West Bank First Trip

TRANSPLANTING (FOR DAVID)

I WAS WITH ONE other leader and forty-seven people—tourist pilgrims on their first trip. My partner did the liturgies, Old Testament background, and history, and I did the gospels, Psalms, and prophets, telling stories for reflection—along with the pragmatics of keeping everyone together (countless countings to account for stragglers. Sometimes like herding cats.)

We arrived back in Jerusalem after four to five days in northern Israel. People were beginning to flag and tempers flared here and there. One woman, in her mid-seventies, had been having difficulties. After some probing, we learned that she was on Coumadin—and had changed her dose just days before the trip. It was Sabbath eve and my immediate job was to find a doctor. We were in a guest house, run by a religious community. No one seemed to be able to provide us any information. But a young woman at the front desk, maybe seventeen, finally after many phone calls said, "My uncle is a doctor." There was a long pause. "But we live in the West Bank. You'd have to come with me when I go home through the checkpoint, meet my uncle in the compound, and then come back with him through the checkpoints to here. He'll come, but it won't be easy. He'll see the woman who is sick, and then you'll have to come back through again with him. And I'll accompany you too."

There were more calls, and the process began. Not too bad the first time through, with my being an American. Then I met her uncle, the doctor whom I learned on our long wait times was in charge of transplants, organ donations, and immediate surgeries in the midst of accidents and attacks for the West Bank community.

We ate some bread and cheese, figs and olives. Then the doctor gathered his bag and IDs and we were on our way. We drove to the crossing point and got out of the van. The soldiers took the van apart, and the searches started, for him and me. Though we told the soldiers he was seeing someone who was sick, we waited more than two hours. Finally, with the van back together and us dressed again, we passed through and returned to the guest house.

The doctor was kind and caring, ministering to his patient. He ordered a prescription ASAP and said that she should go home the next day if possible, necessitating a change of ticket back to New Jersey, then Texas, through Rome. She would need to be met at home by her physician.

Then it was time to return the doctor and his niece through the checkpoints again. (third time for me). And once again, though it was the same soldiers at the same point, there were long lines, waits, stripping down of the van again, and strip searches—this time with body searches. This time I complained. It was more than unnecessary; it was humiliating. I was laughed at and shoved around, and not until hours later were we finally back at the compound where the doctor and his niece and family lived. By now the sun had set, and it was decided not to try to go back for a fourth time the same day. I would stay overnight with them and they'd take me back through another way.

So came an overnight stay with the doctor's family in an old house, unfinished, as are many in the West Bank due to regulations and laws. The first floor was concrete, open on all sides with a small wall along one side. And one light bulb in a corner of the open space. They had prepared and laid out a feast: breads, pita, lamb shanks, olives, greens, hummus, cucumbers, chickpeas, wine, water, crackers, feta, sweets, honey coated nuts. We sat as the day finally cooled. We began with a chanted prayer, and then I listened to them as they talked. They asked me what my desert home in New Mexico was like and found out that we were on the same latitude line half a world away. The children—many of them, a dozen or more all under twelve, played and shyly came forward, told me their names and ages, and asked about my brothers and sisters—the nine of us that were left—and they were curious about how old they were and how the others had died.

Then candles and oil lanterns appeared and were lit, and I noticed after the first round of food had been cleared away and the desserts and wine and coffee came out, a photograph on the table. I walked over and picked it up and carried it with me back where I was sitting, and we started a game. That's you! I'd say and I'd point to the photo—I was mostly right in connecting the faces and the children. There was laughing and giggling when I was wrong (there was a set of twins). I went through them all, and a few adults: aunts, uncles, grandparents, cousins—all smiling back at me as they were noted, named, and acknowledged.

Then I noticed there were two faces that I hadn't found in the group all gathered around me, and I innocently asked, "Who are these two? They're not here tonight? Are they away with relatives or off with others?" There was silence. It descended almost as thick and quickly as the shadows of night came down around us. I glanced up and everyone was looking at me.

After a few moments, one of the children, a boy of about eight said, pointing at one of the missing ones, a boy in the picture: "Oh, that's Reuben, our big brother," and a girl piped up, "And that's our sister Eliza. They're not with us anymore. They were shot by the soldiers. Abba took them to his hospital. But they're still here. We just don't know exactly where."

And the list began: Reuben's eyes went to a Jewish mother; and his liver and kidneys to a boy about his age, and his lungs to a little baby. And Eliza's eyes are in a girl who goes to high school in Tel Aviv, and her heart is in someone else—like her liver. We know they're on the other side of the line, looking back at us when we eat and play and we are together. We look for them when we go out and look across through the fence or when we go to the other side. We look at everyone very closely and see if we can find them, recognize them in someone. We know we'll know if they are there in someone, so they're with us, still just not here right now.

Then one of the younger children, a girl said, "Momma says that you can sleep in Eliza's bed tonight so when you go back over to the other side tomorrow you'll be able to see her if she's around where you are." I was stunned, in tears, as were others among the adults. I did sleep in Eliza's bed that night, honored and wondering what her dreams had been, cut off so suddenly, her young life ripped from her by bullets. And I thought of where her eyes and heart and lungs were—who carries them and sees and breathes because of her life and her being killed—yet not dead for all who loved and cherished her.

The next morning as the children scattered to school, after coffee and yogurt and bread, I went with their father/uncle and some cousins and all the others heading across into Israel for work to another entry point. We bypassed yesterday's checkpoint and slipped through a field, and a back door in a building with its back entrances open so that workers could pass through into the city. I returned to take the older woman with the group home five days early. I never made it to Ein Karem, southwest of Jerusalem where Elizabeth and John traditionally went to hide from Herod's soldiers when he sought the life of all the boy children, looking for Jesus newly born into the world. Today Palestinian women pray there for their children. Both Christian and Muslim, they are devoted together to begging for their children to escape an early and violent death, at a soldier's hands. But I realized I didn't need to go. I'd been to Ein Karem already and had been blessed and taught firsthand the meaning of sacrifice, forgiveness, and resurrection life with its sad joy and bittersweet taste. And I learned the meaning of heart-sight and heart transplanting—taking life from one body and giving it to another, a stranger or enemy who was now friend and family. It is a terrible and awesome way to making peace.

Blind Sight/Hindsight

I WAS STUDYING IN Berkeley at the GTU and UCB—mainly theology, for a PhD. Two days a week I'd take the Bart train from Berkeley into the Tenderloin, an area of San Francisco heavily populated by homeless and street folk. The Franciscans have a huge church there (it is also on the edge of the financial district), St. Boniface, and they run a soup kitchen, services for the homeless, basic medical exams, etc.

For five or six hours, my job was called "the keeper of the bed tickets." When I arrived at 7:30 in the morning, I was given thirty to thirty-five "tickets." They were free passes for one night in one of the "hotels" in the area—as basic you could get and on occasion, flea-ridden, but off the streets and safe for the night. I was supposed to give them out by 1:30 p.m.—latest. But it didn't take long for me to learn that the most desperate and needy ones showed up later—near 4 or 4:30 p.m. These were the elderly and the disabled, especially the week the SSI checks came out, or a woman with a child (or two, sometimes three) who had been working the line for food and clothes, hoping that someone would team up with her—or maybe help her out—to get some diapers, formula, etc. in exchange for company. So, I'd save four or five a day for the stragglers, the latecomers.

It had been a brutal day—the heat near 100, tempers flaring, fights on the line. It was after 5 p.m., and I gave my last ticket to an elderly black man, grizzled beard and hair. He kept kissing my hand in gratitude and I was trying to not cry. I was hot and sticky, like everyone else, and decided that instead of walking the fifteen to twenty minutes to the BART station (the pavement was hot even through my sandals), I'd take the bus.

I got on, took a quick look around and noticed the one seat

left open, paid my fare, and made a beeline for it fast. I slid into it before I looked at who was in the seat beside me. It was a black man, probably in his late forties, early fifties—hard to tell with folks who live on the street. And then I got a whiff off of him and nearly gagged, turning my face to the aisle. I looked up and scanned the others on the bus. I was the only young (under thirty, white, and to them, fairly well-heeled) woman, and I was being eyed by a wide mix of the human race beginning with an older Asian woman directly across from me. There were many Latinos, every range of color—we were a motley crew—all hot, sticky, sweaty, tired and just wanting to go home.

My seatmate was very loaded and very chatty. He immediately started talking to me: "What ya doing on this bus, lady? It's Friday night."

I said, "Going home." And he went on and on. I tried to smile, said a word or two here and there, and was embarrassed. I was being acutely observed by everyone, and everyone was listening in on our talk. The short trip was becoming endless, lengthening by the moment. I didn't want to be rude and cut him off (or maybe I did, but just didn't dare).

And then as he babbled on, I looked down as someone else got on and came down the aisle and then others starting filling up the aisle space—and I noticed his feet. Gross! Filthy—caked dirt, bits of garbage, shit, I'm sure. (Folks on the street have terrible problems with their feet.) He had one old sneaker with a big hole—his toes were sticking out, with blackened nails—and the other foot was bare.

Without thinking—I was flustered—I said, "Oh dear, you lost a shoe! (loud enough for a lot of folk to hear).

He looked over at me and gummed a huge smile and said, "No dear—I found one!" I was stunned, speechless. I have never recovered; a door opened up and I found myself catapulted through it. Earlier that year, in my basement apartment, I'd been in a "rolling, then shaking" earthquake. I was standing on the floor one moment and in the next, I was on the next level—two steps up, about six feet away from where I had stood!

I suddenly knew what the old Irish adage meant: "There is another world but it's hidden in this one." I had just been "parabled," if there is such a verb...a parable that reveals to us and lets us experience for perhaps a moment or two what it's like to live in God's world. I saw that nothing is as it seems or appears to be. There's always another side—perhaps the side that God is on—and looks out and sees us. Now—still—what to do with that sight?

God Lives in
This Neighborhood

T HE POOR ARE ALL those without power, without influence, without rights, those falling through the cracks in society. The poor are welfare recipients and immigrants, all those who are blamed for the economic problems of the day. They are the victims and casualties of violence, those caught in political cross fires, made homeless, landless, nationless. Afterward they are caught in the web of economic injustices that result from war, racial and ethnic hatreds, and religious conflict. They are those who most rely on God's providence and care, for we have abandoned them. They must trust God because they know from experience that they cannot trust us, even those of us who call ourselves faithful believers in God, the God who became human and dwells among us in our flesh and blood. And the poor, those blessed in the Scriptures, hardly know that blessing consciously. More often they are completely unaware of being beloved of God.

I am always struck by a simple devastating memory when I bless the food I am about to eat. One day a couple of years ago when I was on vacation in southern Mexico near the Chiapas border, I had spent the morning with some youngsters talking about the rebels and church, about Bishop Ruiz and the gospel for the following Sunday. I bought lunch for a half dozen of these street urchins, as most people would call them, and one of them said grace. It was a direct hit: "God is great. God is good. God lives in this neighborhood, but you are welcome here." I have never forgotten that experience, and when I eat in so many places around the world, I wonder does God live so clearly in this neighborhood, in my neighborhood?

Nicaragua 1976

I'D BEEN IN MEXICO City and Cuernavaca in 1969 to teach language school. Cuernavaca was still a laid-back, primarily tourist town about sixty miles south of the city: huge cathedral with stark architecture, black stone baptismal font in the entrance, a zocalo/plaza with a fountain. I stayed with a family. Now, nearly ten years later and in Central America, I was helping to lead a group teaching about history during Somoza's reign and the Sandinista's struggle; the rise of the small Christian communities—places for survival, sharing of faith, food, resources, and resistance—how to work for change that was radical. They were seeking political, economic, and social change together using the gospel and the prophets—and to do it with no violence, no retaliation, and no harm.

It was the third day, early morning. The heat hadn't started to rise yet; there was even a small breeze. It was a small town, and we were staying with families that were taking such good care of these visitors—offering gracious, attentive hospitality. I was one of the two leaders with about twenty-four people (studying theology). None of them had been south of the border. We had brought medical supplies: first-aid kits, vitamins, antibiotics, water purifying tools, etc.

I had learned painfully when I'd lived those months in Mexico that when speaking or when eating with anyone, I was never to ask about food, especially: "When was the last time you ate?" I had innocently asked some young children—street kids no more than eight or ten years old in an alley off the main plaza, who were begging—and I thought I'd get an answer like: "A tortilla this morning for breakfast." The answer slapped me sideways—"*Senorita, on Tuesday.*" And it was Friday morning! So, this time, I had brought gifts for the families we were staying with: cans of tuna, jars of peanut butter, dried fruit, oatmeal, energy bars, seeds and nuts. And I would never ask that question again. As always, the guest was served first. And as I ate, I watched the portions grow smaller. I learned the habit that after I'd eaten a little, I'd feign not feeling all that well and pass what was left on my plate to the youngest. The excuse of "Montezuma's Revenge" came in handy—along with laughter.

After breakfast, I went down the main street (not paved) and walked to the small fountain in the zocalo. There were lots of street food venders, children playing, workers moving toward other houses and projects and older women on benches and crates, watching. It was a small bit of a park, with a few trees and bushes. I sat on the edge of the fountain; it was cooler near the spray. And I took my journal out of my side pack. It was new, a blank book, lined and covered in bright colored cloth. It was a good-sized one, 8 x 12, so that I could sketch as well as take notes and journal. I had two and a half days to catch up on since an initial entry on the plane from Miami and a stopover in Belize just sitting and roasting on the tarmac.

I wrote, engrossed, trying to remember: the names of the extended family that I was staying with, initial impressions of Managua after the earthquake; the ride in pickup trucks for hours out into the country and the little town of Estelli where we were, surrounded by small farms, a cooperative. I wrote furiously, making notes in margins on things I wanted to ask about—and words in Spanish and English that I'd heard and wanted to make sure I knew the meanings of. And suddenly I realized it was very, very quiet. The laughter, the yelling, the sound of children, the hum of talk—it was all silent. I looked up to see at least twenty or thirty children right in front of me, staring and pointing. Many of them looked upset, and the women were talking in low voices to one another.

My Spanish was primitive but returning. I said good morning and told them my name, whom I was staying with, and what we were doing here. A few of them responded with their names, asking where I was from and what did I think of their town. Some had heard of New York City and a few of Washington, DC (where I was going to school), and others not at all. I turned my book around so they could see and drew them a fast map of the United States, Central and South America, and Canada, putting in Belize, Nicaragua, Salvador,

Guatemala, Honduras, etc. I asked them what places they knew about and showed them where they were on the map, how far away these places were, and how we got here. They were amazed at how long it had taken for me to get to their town: train to airport, airports to different countries, travel in trucks and on foot.

Then one of them said, "You know you're not supposed to be doing 'that'!" It took a few moments for me to figure out what "that" was—it was writing in a book! They were shocked. I asked questions. Books were sacred. There were so few books, and they were all learning to read; anyone who learned would teach others—even their parents and grandparents. They treated books with great care. If you were allowed to take a book home, it was an honor and you had to protect it; it belonged to everyone.

Then they asked, "What's the name of the book? What's its name?" I showed them that it was a blank book—some pages with lines and some blank to draw on—and that I was writing what would be in the book.

Each one wanted to see it, to hold it. "You mean we can write a book?" I assured them they could. "What are you going to put in it?" I told them I was writing about what was happening; where I was staying; who was teaching us (their community leaders)—and that we were here to learn about them. And I added that I was going to write about them now! All of them! They giggled and laughed. "What are you going to say?"

"I'm going to write about what you're teaching me: how to appreciate words, and books, what power they have to connect and hold people together, to share their dreams and knowledge and work for what everyone needs—for justice. Anything that's important can be put in a book. It helps us remember what we talk about together and learn from one another."

"Oh, like we do with the gospel when we read about Jesus?" came from one of them. (Out of the mouth of babes comes wisdom.)

Then the Spirit must have started kicking in and I asked them, "Would you like to write in my book? I'd like to remember your names...and write a word or two next to your name that you think are words that we all need to know and remember and make come true. You can teach me about you and what you want to do with your lives." And so, for the next hour or two each carefully used my pen (they only had pencils) and wrote out their whole names and a word or two. They were followed by their mothers and grandparents, and just about anyone passing by lined up to sign my book. Many printed their names because they were just learning to write, along with learning to read. (The Sandinistas had begun a literacy campaign throughout the country and in less than six or seven years had dropped the illiteracy rate from over 90% to less than 15%.)

The words, which they painstakingly spelled out, often with help from others, ran the gauntlet: "hope, live, set us free, love, no violence, believe, read, struggle, justice, God with us, share food, rich, poor, Nuestra Senora, El Salvador, El Senor Jesus, mi hijo/ hija, peace, sing, plant corn, eat together, dance, rejoice." And it grew hotter, so we retreated into the church for noon Mass and celebrated. They lifted The Book high with many alleluias. It was, they told me, the first book most of them had seen and read. They learned to read on the Good News to the poor!

This was my first morning in Nicaragua. This was my first lesson and my introduction to God's place among the poor and some of God's friends, surrounded by growing fields. All else that I learned and experienced was built and added onto this foundation. After much embracing and kissing, and many smiles and invitations to come to their homes and eat, everyone went back to what they had been doing and I went home to my family for lunch.

That book is now more than forty years old. The cheap paper and the ink are fading. But it is my treasure—hidden in a field, hidden by a fountain, hidden in the poor friends of God—the best gift ever. It still holds the first tastes of great joy and why I would be willing to "sell everything to get the whole field!"— a community of the people of God intent on uncovering the secret entrances to God's home among us even now.

VISITATION II

ONE WOMAN'S RAGE: ANOTHER PSALM TO THE NAME IN HUMILITY

Newly met friends
A humble Salvadoran woman—
I helped her change out of her stiff, dirty clothes
then take a shower;
she was shaking.
Then I saw
blue welts on the belly of this pregnant woman;
first rage, now grief.

I am ashamed again of being
Goliath moving south, leaving armor and waste
as the old glaciers moved swallowing all in their wake,
a wave on the land.
We practice apartheid in the Americas
but we still call ourselves David
and go on dancing with glee
now on the ark of injustice.
We teach terror, defend evil glibly,
are pragmatists with a club.
Our god demands blood sacrifices
and all the booty of war.
Our myth, our mandate
to destroy in the name of democracy.
We now have our holocaust for history.

Afterward, when she left
I threw up in helplessness.
Then in a psalm of distress cried out—
O God, we are mercenary angels
licking only our own narcissistic wounds;
our innocence is irreplaceable.
To whom do I confess? What good remorse?
What words show forth the shame of my complicity?
I belong to this country of Philistines
and I pray for a slingshot to take us down and leave us in the dust—
and then in death I will await the epiphany of the poor.
They will judge as will the Son of Man, weighing us
within the hand of their want and our greed
for they have suffered unjustly, unduly
and their mercy, like yours, is true.

For now, and until all harm is undone, all I do are acts to repay
her kindness to me;
penitence and alms in remembrance of a woman
who trusted me, her enemy—
named Pia
who smiled and touched my face when she saw
my distress at her old pain.
And I trembled. Today I learned the rabbit's fear,
the wolf's silence at the smell of man, the deer's swift timidity
and now I take my stand with all the small creatures of this earth
the children, the ones widowed by war, the refugee, the ones who
cleave to Divinity knowing all too much of humans' kind.

May our sins end.
My afterthought: oh may that child mend and grow up to be
El Salvador—
 or La Justicia. Amen.
I take refuge in the memory: she hummed in the shower, standing
in warm
water. She blessed my small house with grace.

Who's the Missionary? (Early 1990s)

I T WAS A COURSE on missiology, cross-cultural mission, other religions, and how to preach while being conscious and aware of others' wisdom traditions—how God is already present wherever you were assigned in mission. The underlying intent was to reveal to those getting ready to go overseas and in language school that they were not bringing anything to the people they went to serve; it was they who would draw them into a worldwide view and the web of God's kingdom. It would be the people they were privileged to visit and live with who would upend their world.

The class was crowded, composed of many men and women religious from diverse communities, priests, brothers, and a few laypeople, mission volunteers, and some people just interested in the topics. And it was rough going—not what they were expecting. They were super enthusiastic, zealous and wanting to learn how to evangelize and teach others. They came with an assortment of ideas on community: what it entailed and how to create it but also with the sense that these people needed to be evangelized and that they were going to teach them how to be the children of God, organizing them for the work of justice and making Church. They had many traditional views of what made a missionary—Francis Xavier; martyrs; the Jesuits in North America who came with the colonizers to work with the heathen; Thérèse, the Little Flower; praying for lost souls.

The ideas of what is called "liberation theology" in academic circles were new to them, even as ideas: how to read the Scriptures together in small communities, being called to conversion with others and held accountable by others. The sense that one would accompany the people you were sent to—as the gospel described, "those who followed Jesus and went off in his company." How to stir a sense that they were beginning a journey that would mean they would in a sense "disappear" in order to make room for Jesus to "appear" and that it was Jesus who was waiting for them to arrive and had been with these people long before they came.

There was resistance that built from the first day. It was couched in the language of "individualism." The first word of practically every sentence was "But": "But—I...you don't understand my gifts...this is what I will be able to do...."

There were three South African women in the group who barely spoke, except to one another, for the first eight days (of a ten-day class). Finally, I sat with them after class and we talked. Their English was excellent. They had been educated in mission schools by teachers from the British Isles. They wore simple light-blue long skirts and short veils, their long hair piled up under in twists and knots. They were the only ones in a "habit" in the group. They soon confessed to me that they were sorry they weren't participating very much but they felt so out of place. No one asked them why they were in the class. I had met with them previously and they told me that they were studying theology for degrees in the US so that they could return to their tribes and train their own catechists, theologians, and people to reflect on the Scriptures.

They said they had been talking and knew what "the stumbling block" to feeling like being a member of the class was—they lived and did everything in community. They found it impossible to operate, to do ministry, even to live on their own without others. And they were finding it hard to understand why most thought and expressed their ideas so strongly and singularly. Even more they didn't understand why so many didn't seem to see or even want the absolutely fundamental need for a community to hold you accountable for your choices, your actions, and even your opinions.

There were only two days of class left. Everyone was working on a paper, though I had been clear that they could do any pro-

WHO'S THE MISSIONARY 31

ject they were interested in (preferably with some other members of the class—perhaps those who were going to the same country they had been assigned to). They could use stories, music, mime, photography, anything to express what they were learning, questioning, even disagreeing with as part of their project. One of the three asked, "Can we do a project on community and will you grade us all as one?"

I was delighted and told them, "Of course; yes, please do."

The next morning the three sisters arrived. They were all tall women, over 6'3" and now dressed in their "home" clothes. (They explained that they only wore the habit in the US because it was felt that it was expected of sisters from foreign countries.) They were wrapped in long swathes of cloth with vibrant designs. They looked and walked like huge, graceful free-flowing birds—with more cloth wrapped high on their heads, matching or in contrast with what was folded and wrapped around their bodies.

They took everyone by surprise. I explained that they were doing a project together and all would be graded the same. They stood before the others and began to chant, sing, sway, and move together, and then each did their own steps, weaving in and out. It was the gospel reading for the coming Sunday: the seed sown in the field and when evening came, an enemy sowing weeds among the crop. But—let them grow together. Don't pull out the weeds. They began to mime the words while they sang in their native tongues (three different languages). It had taken me a few minutes to realize it was the gospel—others in the room were looking a bit perplexed—enjoying the music and the dance, but not understanding what text it was—or even that it was Scripture.

And it was vigorous—dance movements, heads bowed, arms thrown back and swung outward. And suddenly one or two people noticed that the main singer was becoming undone—literally. Her wrap had slipped out of its intricate foldings at her back, and a piece was now dragging on the floor. Another's cloth head wrapping was coming loose, and her hair was tumbling down. They were coming apart at the seams, every which way....

And then, gracefully, seamlessly, one moved behind the singer, pulled the loose cloth free, slowly turned her around while she sang, refolded and tucked in the errant piece, and tightened another piece that was dragging free. She, in turn, took off her companion's head cloth, first re-twisting her hair into a tight knot, and then refolded it into the cloth and wrapped her back up. It was part of the dance, and they bowed to one another in thanks.

They finished their song and the gospel presentation, and they spoke, each adding a piece: Community—each of us, all of us are mirrors to one another. Even when we dress at the beginning of the day—we do so by instinct but we need each other to make sure we got it right—that we are together—and we need others to watch us if we are coming loose. Most often we are unaware and don't notice except when it's reached a point of embarrassment and we are awkwardly attempting to put ourselves back together again on our own. It's not just our outward appearance, but it's our souls, our minds and our hearts that need to be kept together, presentable, and work so that one or another doesn't get in the way or keep things from getting done well, in sync. We fill up what's lacking in one another. We each become who we are with one another. We are indebted to those who see us as we can't see ourselves. We are all mirrors.

Then they stood silent.

It was exquisite. Naturally they got an A+++. They were the only ones who received that grade. And I heard myself saying, "Even our God, the Trinity, is community. We look like them, made in their image best, most powerfully and most easily recognized and taken to heart when we are together. The One in the Three and the Three in the One."

For the closing prayer they brought a wild piece of cloth, wrapped me up, piled my hair up (then long and black and thick), and turbaned my head. And they invited anyone else who would like to participate in the dance and music for the rest of the prayer service to be wrapped in their hand-dyed cloths. And we ate together afterward—the food they had cobbled together in their dorm room—their food, their way.

They were the best, brightest, and most engaging expression of community I'd ever seen until then. They taught me, and I think everyone in the class, that we may be able to survive without a community but it will be devoid of and lacking in a grace and Spirit that makes us more truly who we are in God's image and likeness. An undeniable presence of the Spirit is not only joy but diversity in community.

Behold! Do You See What I See?

I SOMETIMES WONDER IF I have ever really seen what is, what is reality. I'm not talking about eyesight, but about insight, or as Gerard Manley Hopkins, the poet, wrote: inscape. What is the inside of something, someone like? What world dwells and resides inside each one of the more than seven billion people on this spinning earth? For the last years I have spent a month or two in the countries of Peru and Bolivia, and I always carry my camera with me to take away what I can see! I used to draw and paint, but then I broke my left hand (I was a lefty) and somehow severed the connection between my eye and my hand and lost that gift.

But in Peru and Bolivia, the indigenous peoples often do not appreciate others taking their picture, especially their faces and eyes, where they carry their souls. They do not appreciate strangers peering deeply into them and taking what was not offered. And I try to respect that when I am among them. So I take lots of pictures of backs, from behind and sideways. And when the film is developed, I am amazed at what I see and what there is still to see as inscape/insight. There are long, thick, and skinny braids. Gorgeous mantas, long shawls that carry everything from babies to thirty pounds of food, firewood, cloth, grasses/wheat/rye, quinoa, amaranth, and even stones, adobe bricks, and flowers for the market. They carry burdens, little infants asleep with rosy cheeks that are the result of cold and wind at high altitudes, over 11,000 feet. There are larger children peering at me sideways, curious and often breaking into smiles when they see me looking at them through this silver/black small box. They look with care, serious and intent. And lowering the camera I look back.

In the market I always begin by taking pictures of hats hanging from the tent rafters, or vegetables, mounds of potatoes, corn and unknown riches, slabs of meat and innards, or wild abandonment of cloth every color of the rainbow, spread out on the grass or walkways. I can see a lot with my telephoto lens and invariably I will look up to see others, especially the women, watching me. They smile. I smile and they look at each other sideways, smile again and turn their backs all together so that I can see and take pictures of their backs, their distinctive hats and weavings. They turn, look sideways at me again and laugh out loud.

On one of the last days that I was in a huge market in a rural area, a woman came up to me (very unusual) and she wanted to look through my camera and see what I could see. She looked a long, long time and then looked at me. Then she stood in one place and turned all the way around, with the camera to her eye, encompassing the world. Her eyes were wide, wider and wider still, as though she was the lens on the camera. She motioned to the others, and one woman took me by the hand, drew me into the group, wrapped a manta over my shoulders (deep rose pink) and fixed my braid (which was very skinny, short and silver in comparison to their rich, night-black thick ones) and she took my picture with all the others. She arranged them, rearranged them, with me, in obvious generation groupings and with friends, sisters, and cousins, and there was much laughing. Then she gave me my camera back, after everyone had a chance to see, to pivot and peer at the world and to take a picture of what they chose to capture (though we all knew they'd never see the pictures developed).

Then she did something remarkable. She pointed to her eye and then touched mine and in rapid fire, Quecha touched my fingers to her throat and her fingers to mine, while all the women nodded strongly in affirmation. I had no idea at all what she was saying, but I did understand something—I'd been drawn into their line of sight, their vision and their world. They gave me potatoes (purple and yellows ones) and corn for our lunch, smiled, picked up their heavily loaded mantas, and turned for home up the mountainsides.

I looked to Victor, my Quecha friend who is also fluent in Spanish and English, and my other friends who are missionaries who have been in the Altiplano for decades, and their mouths were wide open and staring at the women as they left, turning back to smile and wave at us again and again. They translated. She told you that your eye sees the way they see: behind, what is the past that they carry and off to the side, what's outside, lost, on the fringes, the edges—and so you are one of them. And you have the same soul— that was the bit about the throat. It seems they believe, along with the peoples of the Middle East, even at the time of Jesus, that your soul is in your throat. And they talked with their eyes if they couldn't with their throats! I knew I'd been having deep penetrating conver- sations for the past couple of weeks and nary a word was uttered, but so much passed between total strangers that was intimate and speaking reams to me.

An angle of sight! There is a saying that seeing is believing. And many cultures and peoples believe in second sight: someone who has the gift of seeing into one's soul, or into the future, in glimpses, or understanding dreams and what is not spoken, or seeing what earth tells us in the weather, trees, birds, and behind the veils of creation at certain times of the day, usually at dusk and dawn when the light shifts and moves and the air is almost visible. I knew I'd been seeing things, important and crucial things in all those days of watching people, often while they watched me. I'd been learning a language of Spirit, of incarnation and relationship. And I returned to the states seeing my place, my culture, government, economies, faces, and backs through their eyes.

What are we seeing these days, now years since the autumn of 2001? We see squinting, with our eyes almost closed, and we see mistrust, danger, treachery, and violence in anyone who doesn't look like us. We do not look at people, not even sideways, or with insight or inscape. We see and judge and then speak of what is outside and what is strange to us, or just unknown or different. And we see violence often, as the only response to whatever we are feeling and whatever we perceive others doing in the world. And we are told to see that everyone who is not "with us, is against us" (contrary to Jesus' words that "if they are not against us, they are with us"), and to report anything suspicious to authorities, warnings that are posted on traffic signs in major cities and posted in public places. We see so many as "them," and "them" is a code word for all those whom we see as evil, as inhuman, as we presume, self-righteously and even religiously, as not good, like us. Our sight is skewered and off-kilter and we are seeing less and less of what is actually there—what is reality and sadly, who is watching us watch them.

In Trinitarian theology, the world and all its inhabitants and what God has created as good, as very, very good, is called "the sacrament of the Spirit." It teaches that for those who have eyes to see, The Holy is everywhere waiting to be seen, to be recognized, appreciated, drawn into one's soul, in wisdom, insight, and inscape. It urges us to remember and to practice looking back at God who looks at us and sees us in all things/places/faces and eyes. As Meister Eckhart, the Dominican mystic wrote: "The eye with which God sees me is the eye with which I see God." And it follows that "the eye with which we see God is the eye with which we see others, and the eye with which others see us." What are others seeing when they look at us these days? Are we the children of light, the children of peace, of no harm to others; the children who offer to all others sanctuary, refuge, and a star to steer home by? Does our angle of sight turn us around, make us see sideways, see through others' eyes, see behind and far forward, see with God's eye?

It is time to learn the art of seeing and speaking without words, to touch our enemies and others' eyes and throats with our fingertips and to smile, welcoming, respectful, careful to not steal or take what is not given to us and to see ourselves as others in the world perceive us. Our prayer these months of fading light, dying and falling must be: "Lord, please, that I may see." Lord, please, that we, who call ourselves Christians, may be seen for what we are and not turn away from your gaze upon us. Lord, please, may we see everyone in the light of your eyes and glance upon all the children of earth with compassion and wonder at all whom you have made in your image." It is time for a new angle of sight: insight, inscape, from behind the eyes of the Holy One who dwells among us, in all of us by Incarnation. "Lord, please, open our eyes!" Amen.

Dogs

G ROWING UP, WE HAD pets. There was a real variety, an assortment—gerbils, birds, fish, rabbits, and once—a couple of weeks after Easter Sunday—we were awakened to early crowing. To everyone's surprise, especially my father's, it was obvious that one of the cute chicks in our baskets was a rooster! Cats were outlawed, but of course, there were dogs—mostly mixes and mutts, rescued from the pound. They all had their quirks. One would go upstairs but wouldn't come down and had to be carried (she weighed at least thirty pounds). Another would get in the car and loved riding with his head out the window, but getting out—no way. They were definitely like members of the family. In one of my sister's wedding albums, Sandy, a white shaggy dog who was gorgeous, is in every picture taken at the house before the ceremony—and she went with my sister as part of her dowry. Her husband got the dog too.

There were only two rules with regard to the dogs, and they were strictly enforced. No dogs in any bed—ever—and no feeding of the dog from the table. They'd all eat practically anything offered them and whatever might be left out on tables, counters, etc. There was only one thing not a one of them would touch—oatmeal. We ate Navy oatmeal (it arrived in fifty pound bags) from October to May. It was "gross." No matter what we doctored it up with—raisins, honey, brown sugar, milk—ugh. Wads of it on spoons, even whole bowls would surreptitiously be slipped under the table, to be met only by a whine or a pathetic whimper—no quick wet tongue on your hand—followed by a quick rebuke from my father. The guilty party would have to clean up after the dog for a week and take out the garbage for the week too.

Why all this about dogs? In the late 1990s, I was doing a parish mission on the east coast. Along with giving nightly talks and speaking at all the liturgies, I would often be asked to do an evening for high school students or shorter sessions in the morning for those who didn't want to come out at night. Then one time I was asked to do an hour and a half with middle schoolers (grades three to six)—over 300 of them!

We were talking about Jesus. I gave them some background on what it would be like at Jesus' age (and their own ages) to live under Roman domination and that he probably worked with Joseph six days a week and walked with him to the construction site—about four to eight miles. And that the Sabbath day was sacred and they lived from one to the next, reading the Scriptures about the Messiah who would set them free. They were especially interested when we talked about Joseph and that it was Joseph who would have taught Jesus everything (that was the way Jewish society and families were set up). He would have taught him his prayers, how to be a Jew, what was expected of him by the time he was twelve (bar mitzvah when he became an adult), the learning of the Torah portion that he would chant and preach on, and all the commandments—their history of suffering and persecution as they waited in hope.

They were entranced. A group of five or six of them sitting together were talking, and finally one of them raised his hand. I called on him and he said, "Can we ask you a question? It's not exactly about this but we all want to know."

Inwardly I normally panic at these sort of introductions to questions, but I took a breath and said, "Sure."

"DID JESUS HAVE A DOG?" Uh-duh. I said a little something about hunger and poverty and how poor he was and that people didn't have pets back then—not like we do now—unless they were really rich. They were undeterred. "Could he have had a dog?"

I asked them what they thought, and so for about ten minutes they had a discussion and were hotly engaged in this weighty theological issue. Then—OK—what did they think? First response: "Well God, Jesus' Father, made everything—like all the animals. So, HE obviously likes them all—yes? (An aside: "And two of them made it into the ark." Then they wanted to know if it was only two dogs or two kinds of each dog?!)

Second response: They had decided that if Jesus was growing up and was like them he'd like dogs, even if it would mean that he had to feed them. "Didn't they have sheep dogs to protect from wolves and thieves?"

Third response: Someone said, "We heard this story in church a couple of weeks ago—about this lady—she wasn't a Jew like Jesus. And Jesus was traveling. He wasn't at home; he was visiting another country. And she came and begged and begged and wouldn't go away; she wanted him to heal her daughter (they didn't say what was wrong with her). It was the girl's mother, not her father, who followed Jesus and his disciples, crying out and making a scene. (Maybe she was a single mom?) Do you remember that story?" I told them, yes, I did.

So I told it to them again. And we got to the part they wanted to talk about; they were all into it now: She's on Jesus about her daughter and he says: "It's not right to throw the food of the children to the dogs." So we talked about that. They were divided about whether or not Jesus was being mean to her or was just saying what was true: that dogs don't get fed first—children do, especially the poor). Besides Jesus didn't know her at all. He was a stranger there.

Then we talked about the woman's answer back to Jesus: "Yes, Lord, but even the dogs eat the scraps of food that fall from the Master's table." They got into that—I said, "Go for it." They came back with—"Hey, if it's on the ground, it's up for grabs. Even if it was thrown at the dog to make it go away and stop begging, that would be good too."

And then someone said, "If it was Jesus, I'd take anything I could get from him. I wouldn't care if it was something that nobody else wanted. (I was speechless.) They all agreed. So I told them that was exactly what had happened with Jesus. He'd been teaching and telling stories and helping people in his own town and all around, but most people didn't want to listen to him or, if they did, they weren't doing what he said they should, if they were God's children.

They had another discussion: "OK, what do you think now?"

First response: "Jesus must have been really hurt and disappointed with so many people—especially his friends and neighbors and family.

Second response: "Maybe he thought this lady was just like all the others—she'd get what she wanted and go away too."

Third response: "Maybe she loved her daughter so much, she'd do anything to get her help. And Jesus would like that—it is how he loves us!"

Fourth Response: "Yeah—Jesus was impressed. She was cool with it and getting him even more than the disciples who just wanted Jesus to make her shut up and go away and leave them alone."

One boy said, "I'd sit under the table or be on the ground beside Jesus and take whatever he gave me. I'd eat from his hand. And I bet you, knowing Jesus, it would be good stuff—a piece he broke off special for me."

A lot of them had dogs. So another discussion ensued. This time on what the relationship is between you and your dog. They talked about service dogs. There were a couple in their school that helped students who were in danger of falling, or blind or had diseases and needed a warning to take insulin or eat something when they were going to get sick.

Their dogs were their best friends—always waiting for them to come home, jumping up and down and licking them and asking for a treat—even lying down beside them when they were sad or lonely and sometimes protecting them from bullies and growling at people who were mean to them.

So time was almost up. The question came again: "Well, did Jesus have a dog?"

It was unequivocally YES! Definitely he had a dog—in fact, he probably had more than one—like a pack that followed him around, and he probably told the disciples to be nice to them, not kick them or make them go away, and to share their food with them. So that theological question was solved by the Spirit in them!

After they all left, I was thinking about this story of Jesus and the Syrophoenician woman. Which one is the dog hiding under the table? Is it the woman begging on behalf of her child whom she left at home, desperate for her to live?

Or is it Jesus begging for us to take food from his hand intimately, so familiar, so close, so at ease with us? Is it Jesus, or even the Father, so faithful, wanting to stay with us even when we are pushing him away and don't want to be bothered? Is it our God willing to play and sit panting beside us?

Years later, I gave a dog, a Lhapsa Apso, to a cloistered community as a gift; and one of the sisters, an artist, drew a picture of Kenna (in Tibetan it means "Who?") sitting at the feet of Jesus, with the caption: *Lord, I am content to sit at your feet and I'll take anything that falls from your hand.* They were delighted to think of being Jesus' lap dog

Lap dog or watch dog faithfully trailing the shepherd and trying to keep the sheep together, sounding the alarm, living close to the shepherd in the fields. So—did Jesus have a dog? Today: Does Jesus have a dog? What name does he call you by?

Good Witch, Bad Witch

I HAVE ON A number of occasions been called a witch, sometimes half in jest and sometimes in deadly seriousness—so I've been dubbed both a good witch and an evil one, depending on the person and circumstances. I was told by an eight-year-old boy years ago that I was a good witch; he informed me that good ones only do really good stuff for other people and make people think twice about what they're doing and what's really going on. I thought that was rather astute for being eight years old. He was sure I was one: I had given his family an amaryllis bulb and told him how fast it grows and how it can have one, two, or even three flowers on it. It was an Advent gift. Then I told him when it "died," to cut it all the way down to the dirt and put it in a dark place and it would come back again. He was skeptical but he did it. (He put it in his closet along with sneakers and hockey stick, etc. and left it there.)

One day about nine months later, he happened to find it in the back of the closet and it was growing! It already had a long stalk and two big buds! He ran into his parents' bedroom (Saturday morning, early—much to their surprise—and informed them that I was coming and would arrive that day. What were they doing not getting ready?!). There was much awkward laughter and scrambling, and they tried to explain that I wasn't coming. But I did—I had decided to surprise them. He waited on the front lawn all morning and welcomed me at 3:30 p.m. He told them excitedly, "See, I knew she was coming. She told the flower to bloom so we'd know!"

A most amazing child! He was also convinced I could make it rain, or bring the sun out, and make rainbows appear whenever we would go to the Lake. I told him repeatedly I didn't do those things. Never bought it.

He brought me flowers for coming to visit them once, and when the lady at the checkout in the grocery store asked him who they were for—his mother?—he said, "No, they're for my friend who is a witch." That got her! His mom was with him, cracking up, and she heard him tell the woman not to worry; I was a good one. He explained, when asked, how he knew. The story has lasted long; he's grown now, married and with kids of his own. Haven't seen him in more than twenty years. But I think he was right. There is a streak in me that's a bit witchy—hopefully always good! Wow; got started...hope that makes you smile!

He Gave Me the Stars!

ARLY MORNINGS, PITCH DARK, before 3 a.m., we had meetings before Matins, to have our star lessons. (He was an engineer by study, an astronomer by avocation, and a monk by vocation). We'd stand, in the mountain fastness— no lights to blur the vast array—our heads thrown back, and he'd point out constellations and the Milky Way, and name the stars and planets. He was teaching me how to see, looking at angles, or sideways—at configurations, in all seasons, with the moon waxing and waning through its monthly shifts.

The night was bright with eyes—a world up there, out there, always there…waiting to be discovered, discerned, in layers of clouds, mysteries, holes in the sky. Novas, nebulas—miniscule what we could see. Later I was reading Carl Sagan and was shocked by a statement— that all the data coming back from the Hubbell and other telescopes strung out across the globe, with information streaming into computers (they'd been mapping the universe for years, plotting distances, naming and monitoring satellites) came down to one astonishing fact that just blew their minds, even as calculations kept reinforcing its reality: From what we can see—looking at the map of the universe consistently growing in details—97.9% of the universe is invisible! ("What the hell do we know about anything?" was Sagan's reflection.) I spent two weeks over one Christmas studying pictures from the Hubbell telescope—pouring over a huge coffee-table-sized book, which when laid flat was like two great doors opening before me).

Soon I had stars in my eyes. When I'd close my eyes to pray, meditate or just seek to stop my mind (often like sheep spreading out, scattering across Irish hillsides), I'd see stars, galaxies, smears of light. It was humbling, awesome, casting radiance across darkness— or shining from within it, from behind what my eye could see and perceive. I have always loved the night (dawns, dusks, light fading and tentatively approaching, growing feeble becoming enveloped by a darkness that one could learn to see through and in.)

He gave me the stars, introduced me to the Lord God Master of the Universe—that was in essence one song, one poem, one psalm beyond that enveloped earth (which I so dearly love and am attached to). That world slipped into my small world—like the back of a mirror, allowing me to see beyond, into a direction beckoning, a spaciousness beyond measuring, stretching any sense of who our God might be!

And stars sing! My ears became attuned to these silent muses resounding, humming, thrumming, surging, and receding. I'd close my eyes and I was on the verge, the edge of that sweet abyss, the unfathomable, the void that God held as surely as he holds our small lives and the orb, the ball we call "world" (as a child holds a treasured toy in his hand, wanting to throw it, to play with it, with exuberance and power, with another to catch it). Far away echoes murmuring, enticing me over the edge, out there into the unknown, the invisible, indivisible One—Lord God Keeper of the all the Worlds that is the Father's flesh in Jesus, their Spirit breathing through space and whispering in our souls.

He gave me the stars, the night irresistibly, and I fell in love wanting to dissolve and disappear into such hole-ness, completely. The moon was the first mystic I ever met—the pattern of living and the slow dance—aborning, dying, rising—a serenity, calmness ,and vast strength; the source of secret revelations, transfigurations, ceaseless comings and goings, appearances and disappearances. What grace there is in each created thing, each creature, including each of us—in our shadows and shining solemn depths. I would get lost in the stars and their lighthearted invitations, their nothingness, causing me to tremble with fear, attraction, magnetism, anticipation—being ready at any moment even to fall and streak across the sky. The night sky smiles at us miles up, and it weeps silent tears streaming, streaking in a flash before our eyes.

Contemplating the stars (first lesson of looking at reality with love for me) taught me some of the essential energies of existence, sentience, breathing, being transparent, reflective, ethereal yet eternal, exuding ever and ever their pulsating steadiness. Beyond or in living and dying—space mirrors Divine oneness, asking for surrender, inviting communion. It became Grace (another word for Spirit) unfolding, embracing. It is easy to get caught in this, and ask: "Is this dying into You? Indwelling as You do, the Holy Three—is this a glimpse of your glory?"

Over decades I sought a house with many windows, not just for letting in the light of day, but windows on the sky—not skylights, but open spaces for night prayer and the company of the Star Keeper. For a while I was entranced with their names and meanings: Pleiades, Orion, Aldebaran, Altair, Cassiopeia, Vesperas, plain-named Morning Star, Milky Way, and all those myriad unnamed and unknown ones (except by God who knows them as intimately as he knows each one of us).

He gave me the stars. He gave me eyes to know you and how you keep your loving gaze upon us in all ways. With his wisdom of the night he urged me, who is so bound to flesh and incarnation, to seek how to love and kiss You, The Infinite One. He made me, at my roots, what he sought to be, a monk.

> *For this reason I kneel before the Father, from whom every family in heaven and on earth is named, that he may grant you in accord with the riches of his glory to be strengthened with power through his Spirit in the inner self, and that Christ may dwell in your hearts through faith; that you, rooted and grounded in love, may have strength to comprehend with all the holy ones what is the breadth and length and height and depth, and to know the love of Christ that surpasses knowledge, so that you may be filled with the fullness of God. (Ephesians 3:14 – 9)*

(For Joseph, who watches the stars from the other side now, November 2018)

Light Within Light

PART I

MY FRIEND WAS A photographer, working for NGO's (non-governmental organizations loosely connected to the United Nations). He would cover places around the world—usually in disaster areas where the organizations would respond. The pieces were to inform as well as hopefully elicit donations for the work—providing food, shelter, emergency medicine, relief, etc. during and after evacuations and rescue missions—the result of earthquakes, typhoons, hurricanes, tsunamis.

It was the early 1980's and he was sent to Ecuador. Usually he would arrive in the place, gather his camera gear and head out to survey the area, the extent of damage geographically in regard to water, food, medical survival, and immediate rescue operations. He would look for someone whose story he could tell primarily in photographs: a couple or a family, a single individual—a young child, an elderly person or a parent who had lost spouse or children.

Ecuador, in the years prior to this trip, seemed to be on a continuing run of disasters. They were often termed "acts of God,' and there were purely man-made ones that aggravated other events. First there was an economic collapse and debt crisis with the US interfering and insisting that the government pay its debt regardless of the local hardship—otherwise they would impose further sanctions. The government complied and levied taxes on heating and cooking oil and medicines. Almost immediately, a cholera epidemic hit sections of the country. Drought followed; the coffee crop (mostly exported) failed, and then the rains came—too late.

There were torrential rains resulting in widespread massive flooding and landslides sweeping down the mountains and taking whole villages in their swath. That's when he arrived in an out-of-the-way village, utterly destroyed.

Devastation reigned. It was hot. The ground was a sea of mud, drying fast, caked thick on everything. All vegetation was gone—a few scraggly bushes were bent low; no trees remained. The adobe houses were in various stages of disintegration, mostly collapsed. The scene was one of the worst he had ever witnessed. The food trucks had arrived—two or three days now after the initial walls of water, mud, and debris had torn down into the town. Tents, sleeping bags, water, and emergency teams were set up. He looked around for someone to photograph; to make the centerpiece of how he would try to personalize the general destruction. Everyone seemed dazed, wandering about, in shock. They were streaked and caked with mud, in clothes torn by the force of the landslides and escape.

Then he saw her. She was young, maybe ten or eleven. Her face was thickly coated with dry grey mud, her eyes were darting around; her hair caked and ratted, clothes torn, no shoes. She was on the line—the very long line that snaked along what was left of the main unpaved road behind the food truck. They were sorting and dividing up rice, beans, tortillas, corn flour, bananas, infant formula. There was something about her. He noticed she kept watching the line inch forward toward the food but that her eyes kept returning to the side of the road a bit of a ways away. He followed her gaze, getting closer to her as unobtrusively as he could (he'd learned it was better if the person didn't know they were being photographed and singled out).

She was watching a small clump of children, younger than herself—three of them: a boy about eight; another boy a few years younger, and a tiny girl around two or three. They all looked as she did—forlorn, lost, a layer of dried mud on them, no shoes, huddled together, protectively, under what had been a bush just a bit taller than they were; no leaves, no real shade from the rising heat, but there was a piece of tin propped up beside them. She would nod to them, mouth unspoken words, and then turn and move toward the truck. No one else existed except them—and her—in their small world.

He'd been there, he realized, a couple of hours and already from his position and overview he realized that the truck was running out of supplies. Less and less was being apportioned and given to each person and yet the line stretched out. What would happen when she got there? He moved in, took a few pictures from a relatively safe distance setting up the scene with her, and began to see everything from her vantage point as well as his own longer-distance one. Then she reached the truck's flatbed at long last. She held out hands to the people above her who were doling out the food. It was pathetic. She was handed one small banana—all they had left. People realized there was nothing else left and they just sat down in the road or wandered off looking for shade, waiting for the next truck to arrive. He watched her.

She took the banana carefully and thanked them and bowed and moved, very quickly, back to her little waiting group. He ran to keep up with her; trying to get an angle with the right light. She stopped, and the four of them stood in a small circle together. She said something. He stopped and looked—gawking while they crossed themselves very carefully and they said grace! Then she broke the banana into three pieces—the largest one for the smallest girl child, and then two almost equal ones for the boys. And they slowly ate, taking tiny bites out of their piece of the banana, chewing and chewing slowly. And she, she sucked on the banana peel! He was stunned—by what she was doing, what they did. But suddenly there was something else he became aware of--it was LIGHT. It was the only way he could describe it. It came from within her and enfolded all four of them. He stared at her, her face—which was shining. And he realized: he was seeing transfiguration—radiance shining through this disheveled little girl child, caked in dry cracking mud, in the midst of horror, death, and physical destruction. And she was shining and all was holy. And then it was gone. It was just dry mud, in unholy heat, poverty and human misery, and he felt himself collapse on the ground and found that he was weeping, uncontrollably. After a while he pulled himself together and realized he hadn't taken even one picture since before she was given that one small banana.

Later when he would try to tell the story, his own face would be filled with light and his voice would crack and fill with awe, even fear, and he'd end by saying: "I will never forget her face. And I want to learn to live in such a way that—that light comes through me."

PART II

In the mid 1970's, the Eucharistic Congress was held in Philadelphia. Folks like Dorothy Day and Dom Hélder Camâra (the Archbishop of Recife, Brazil) were speakers. Dom Hélder was a small, almost frail, slight man, going bald, with twinkling blue eyes (on occasion described as a teddy bear), but in reality a man of unusual strength and integrity and fierce love of the gospel and the poor. He lived in a small set of rooms attached to the cathedral, and lived and worked in the favelas, and slums. He was known to be their defender and advocate and the protector of those who preached Good News to the poor. He had been threatened with violence, even death often (he was in his seventies). Already he was known for a famous line: 'When I give alms to the poor they call me a saint but when I ask why there are so many poor, and call for justice, they call me a communist."

It was at one of the liturgies in a local parish downtown. The church was a huge auditorium and it was jam packed. On the stage, musicians from Haiti, the Caribbean, Jamaica and Central and Latin American countries, dressed in their native colors and headdresses, flowing skirts, and shirts were playing: drums, maracas, marimbas, flutes, pipes, etc. The whole building was shaking and everyone was dancing, moving, singing—making a 'joyful noise until the Lord,' as Dom Hélder described it in his homily—and he was singing along with them. The musicians and the people would answer his words, back and forth, responding in song, refrains to the gospel and his preaching.

Then the main musician, a man way over six feet tall, with dreadlocks and a strong voice, moved over to Dom Hélder (who was maybe 4'10" and white haired) and grabbed him, drawing him into the dancing among the musicians, handing him a tambourine—and the music began again. All this was recorded in black-and-white movie film, and what follows is on that piece of film, though I've never been able to find a copy. I saw it a half dozen times almost fifty years ago. The camera follows the black musician and the seemingly frail man in a white soutane and then zeros in on Dom Hélder's face and movements as he sings, hums, and shakes his tambourine. And very gently, beginning a process that is remarkable—he is first an aging man in his seventies and he changes. He is transformed. He gets younger! You can see it happening. He's fifty, then in his forties, thirties, twenties; then younger still, a young man, a young boy and then a child. Then he has the face of a baby! He is shining, even in black and white—radiant, joy streaming from him. It lasts a moment or two and then the process reverses—and he returns to being Dom Helder in his seventies, an elderly man singing, swaying to the rhythms, and praying. Again—a transfiguring moment when a veil is lifted and LIGHT emerges unmistakably for all to see.

PART III

Vancouver Island, British Columbia, a French speaking parish. It's a tiny place that holds maybe seventy to eighty people on Sunday. The pastor preaches in French and English. He's a retired missionary from West Africa. After sixty-plus years in a number of countries, there he finds himself in an enclave of French speakers in English Canada. He's roly-poly, a bear of a man, bald, with eyes that are always laughing, my friend in his eighties now. After daily Mass (I visit from the States) there is tea, coffee, crumpets, and biscuits in the vestibule. He's still in his vestments—flowing bright African colors and stole. It's a feast day and the usual gathering are sipping tea and chatting.

My friend bends down to talk and listen to an old woman in a wheelchair. He draws close to her to hear, and then turns to speak so she can hear him. I'm across the room, a good forty feet away, and I catch sight of them. They are intent, even intimate, smiling, a bit of laughter. And I see it—the LIGHT is emanating from both of them, haloing around them. I'm caught off guard. I'm staring and moving toward them without thinking, drawn like a magnet. They whisper and he holds her frail arthritic hands and they are silent together—eyes closed, praying. I'm close now. They are oblivious to all around them. And then it's gone and they are just two old people talking with one another after church. No one else seems to have noticed. As I look around I realize all has been hushed, stilled, and now the noise level returns to "normal."

And I've been blessed. I was allowed a glimpse of transfiguration and invited to gaze on the glory of the Lord shining through their faces and bodies, invited into another world. The Irish have a saying (from a poet) "There is another world but it is hidden in this one" and sometimes it leaks through, slips out. It is a gift beyond compare, a moment of pure grace. A revelation of Truth when God is made flesh and is dwelling among us in our flesh, in another's flesh—there, for those who are given to see. Once glimpsed, one is God-haunted ever-after with the desire to live so as to reveal that glory, even for a moment here and now. But always it's a gift for another to see. It is a make or break point. Afterward the only question is how to return the favor of those eyes, that face, that human body—that LIGHT, so others can be caught forever in the glance of God among us.

Myanmar (Burma)

I WAS INVITED TO Myanmar, long known as Burma, in the early years of 2000—for the first time, before the Saffron Revolution, when the military attacked the monks and people, killing, imprisoning and torturing them en masse. Myanmar is more than 90% Theravada Buddhist. Religion is steeped in every aspect of culture and life. Practically everyone becomes a monk for a period of time when young—as young as five or six through their formative years for schooling and community life, until they are fifteen or sixteen. Most then leave to become "house-holders"—to live, study, work, marry, and have families—though many remain as monks.

Every morning they all go out begging for food. The streets of every village, town, and city are filled with their saffron and reddish, burnt umber robes. They carry rounded begging bowls of wood, good sized to collect bananas, rice, fruit, any kind of food. They receive the donations with silent bows. It is understood that they in exchange will pray for those who give. By late morning they all return to the monasteries to chant, pray, eat their primary meal of the day together, and listen to teachings. In the afternoon, they work.

Catholics are a tiny minority of the population but relations between bishops and the abbots of the monasteries are very cordial and close. When I visited, we spent a day at a monastery with more than 1000 monks so that I would get a feel for daily life. When the revolution was in full swing, thousands of monks were displaced. They took off their robes (buried them), and the bishops and people took them in, working together to hide them and integrate them into daily life, work, and their homes, protecting them from the soldiers and imprisonment and death.

While I was there for more than six weeks, I began in the south Rangoon and stayed in the seminary, teaching and conducting retreats, and then moved onto the north to do priests retreats and meet with the people and religious communities. I was taken around by a priest and a layman with whom I became good friends, admiring their stamina and their rapport with so many scattered peoples. They would take me to outlying villages, to hill tribes, to stay overnight or for a few days. I would meet with the people, in outdoor schools held after hours from the state schools, and listen to them, and then tell stories.

Henry and his wife Helen were the ones I was with the most, and their ten children. It took me a while to learn (from neighbors) that not all of them were theirs by birth. Two had been left on the side of the road to die—girls—and they were taken into the family. Two were orphaned, their parents killed, from their own village. And another just showed up and was accepted in too. So the ten children and parents lived together. I stayed with them on occasion, more often than with others. They shared their food, their beds, and their life with me. When it was time to leave, I told them I wanted to give them a gift—we could go into town on market day and I could get whatever they needed: cloth, thread, food, utensils. I'd seen some of the most exquisite weavings and young women, especially, sitting at huge outdoor looms for hours each day. At night they would sleep under the bench and begin again as soon as it was light. I was told it took about a month to weave a bolt of the fabric. And always there was an elderly woman with young children, sitting in the dirt close by, spinning the fine, silken thread. This continued no matter the weather. Most buildings had three sides to them at most.

Helen (practically every adult woman I met in the village shared the same name! I was told it was the name of the local headman of the tribe's wife and it was expected that girl children be named after his wife. It had been the custom for as long as they could remember.) Helen and Henry talked it over—what to allow me to give them. I had learned to be politely cautious but clear—Would they prefer money to buy bulk rice, grain or seed, etc.? But it was Helen's idea what they came up with—we would like for you to go with Henry to the market and get us a water buffalo! This was not what I expected at all! But that's what they thought would be best put to use. With a water buffalo they could plant another two fields, hire people in the village to cull and harvest the rice, and after having enough food for their families, have more leftover to sell in the marketplace to buy books, pencils, school supplies, and something only they wanted. So—a water buffalo it was—named appropriately after the donor! We met and I got to see it 'her' opening the furrows of the first new field.

At the end of my visit, of course, there had to be a feast, with dancing, music, story-telling and food. I was given gifts of cloth, wooden statues of seated and reclining Buddha, and a spirit house intricately carved. But at the end of the evening, Helen approached me (she was about forty-two) and gave me a gift wrapped in a rice bag. "This," she said, beaming, "is our family's gift to you." I opened it—it was a large tablecloth—white, hand loomed (made by her family) with red, black, and green designs all along the edges. It was for a long table that would seat ten to twelve people more than adequately. Then she blushed a little and said, "This was our wedding gift from our parents. It is traditional, given down from generation to generation. I'm sorry, but if you look, there are a few stains I couldn't get out; it has been used for birthdays, christenings, funeral feasts, Christmas, all our special occasions. It is for you. You can cover up the stains with a dish or some flowers."

I wanted to refuse and say, "No, please; keep this in your family," but I couldn't. I had to take it, graciously, with deep bows, tears all around, and then embracing. It is the gift from Myamar that I kept the longest. Years later I gave it away to a group halfway round the world from Asia, another continent, for a newly built chapel. (The old one had been torched by the military.) It was their new altar cloth. The clay wine cup and the bread basket nicely covered the tell-tale stains of others rejoicing and celebrating together. And so, it passed on to another generation of believers, another family of God's children in the far-flung kingdom of shared hope and life.

Gifts were given and kindnesses exchanged, faith and lives shared—a water buffalo with a distinctively Irish name and an heirloom tablecloth from the Kachin tribe. Some gifts keep on moving and giving, filled with the grace of the givers.

She Listened

WHEN I WAS GROWING up I was always reading, always escaping to a place of silence, a place of quiet. There were eight of us, sometimes as many as eleven sharing space with "the girls" upstairs in two rooms and "the boys" downstairs, along with my parents. Early on I made a space in the corner of the basement (unfinished). I collected books (my dad brought home a box of used books every Friday evening after work). Books were everywhere—under the beds, stacked in corners, even in the bathrooms. And my lair was constructed of books—three walls with an opening under the stairs. Old rugs, a flashlight, pillows and of course, more books.

I read my way through classes in school, after school, and after homework and chores. I read my way through time, history; went around the world in prose and poems; then out into the universe with science fiction and astrology; then threw in heavy literature, mysteries and whatever looked interesting in the boxes my dad brought home with him. By the time I was in the eighth grade, I was adept at reading a book strategically placed under a notebook, no matter the topic we were studying—religion laced with a novel; geography with poems, science with adventure, and biographies of the famous, infamous, saints and rogues—until she came.

A new teacher, she was probably only ten to twelve years older than us. She was a young sister, but she was intent and dedicated to teaching us, come what may. I scrimped on math and science, more heavily engrossed in words. I got caught—often—and after school was told to pay attention and to concentrate on what was at hand— this subject for this period of time—and to stop escaping reality and all around me by opening another book (any book). I chafed and groused, but she was relentless and she was good. When I started listening, I found she intrigued us with math, science, and problems to solve; she introduced us to another way of seeing, hearing, and coming at things from new angles, opening other worlds. I was caught early on in that last year of grammar school.

At home there were a lot of us and a new baby, chores to do, lunches to make, uniforms to iron, meals to help prepare, and babysitting the others, most of them younger than I. I'd been putting words, ideas, concepts, dreams, wonderings, meanings, and questions in my head for as long as I could remember, but I didn't talk all that much. It didn't seem like anyone really listened. I didn't know it but I was starved for attention: someone to hear me, listen to me, care about what was going on in my head and heart. I started to stay after school even when I graduated and went into high school, about a mile or two away. I'd come back and catch her, after school. We'd sit in a small room off the auditorium that served as a church. It was called the "cry" room for families with children, and it had a door that led into the convent—an in-between place.

She listened for hours, for days, and then for years on end. Home was hard. It was crowded with all the usual tensions, squabbles, arguing with parents overburdened with so many of us, and she listened. Then the talk became questions, philosophy, meaning, future options, God-stuff, who am I—why? It was all the unanswerable issues. I do not remember any specifics or anything she ever told me but I know what was crucial: she listened.

Later, studying theology I was struck by the beginnings of the gospel, especially Mark. As Jesus came up out of the water, he heard a Voice that told him, revealed to him who he was at his root: "You are my child, my servant, my beloved. I take great delight in you" (cf. Mark 1:11, echoing Isaiah 42:1). He was heard. He was accepted, acknowledged, confirmed and told the truth. Then there were the wings of the dove moving and descending upon him and staying— that led him out of the waters and into the world. He was claimed by his Father, inspired by the Spirit, and he—the Word of God made flesh—set out on his life for others. He was God-sent, God-centered, God-ed—obeying his inner truth. He listened and went forth to listen. The foundational meaning of the word—to listen—is to obey, to obey one's deepest reality. It is, it was the onset of the Good News to the poor—about who we are before God, and with and for God. It was the first expressions about the Trinity—communication, communion, words, no words, all languages that bind and bespeak truth.

Later, studying Hebrew and picking up core words and connections, I discovered the phrase "Bat Kol," literally meaning "Daughter of a Voice" (also an echo, inaudible, yet vocal, a revelation, leading to reception, the gift of listening) and was struck dumb with awareness. My friend was Bat Kol—daughter of a voice. She too was doing what Jesus did. He heard the Voice speaking to him (the Voice in the earlier Testament, now so personal and intimate and life-enhancing) and she had heard that Voice herself—was listening all the time. And so, she heard my voice, stumbling, often garbled, seeking to understand, learning to speak, discovering that I too, had a voice. I was given a word from that Voice and on my way, a human voice that echoed God's incessant whisper in all voices, in all things.

Now more than sixty-five years later, she is in her mid-90s and I suspect she is still listening, a Daughter of a Voice, to many others, setting them free to become the word of God spoken in their flesh. Once being heard, you must listen and obey with others, revealing the Voice's truth, and seeking to live so that our God, Three in One takes great pleasure in each of us, all of us, echoing the word seeded in us at our conceptions. She listened and set free my own voice, a gift that could only be given thanks for by passing it on, and on and on—adding to the echo of the Voice.

(In gratitude for Dolores)

The Spirit She Blows
Where She Will

A woman facing chemo and cancer
Her seven-year-old daughter clinging to her;
She'd come to church, an out-of-state visitor.
They loved the music—as high pitched and sometimes
    off-key as it was—she needed the voices.
Not Catholic—quick to say—I'm Protestant.
She hadn't gone to communion though her daughter
got in line and then was frightened when
the lady with the bread tried to bless her.
She hurried back to her mother's side.

Then everyone else was leaving and we started talking.
I gave her the paper with a prayer—she was so grateful.
Said she was going home tomorrow.
Without thinking, I noticed off to the side of the altar
a few of the group "consuming" the leftover bread in
a corner not far from us. I went over—after putting my
hand on her arm—and said: Stay.
I was a visitor to this church too, but local and known
—and I was white.
Went to the group and asked for two pieces of bread.
Eucharist—for being thankful...

Took them and came back, broke them apart and gave
her one and a smaller piece to the little girl and me, the other.
As she ate it I hugged her—no I held her.
Said I would remember her—seemed the right thing to say.

As we went out, standing next to the fountain
I took water on the tips of my fingers—almost shook it at them—
Playfully—but instead blessed both of them with your sign
on their foreheads, lips and heart. They were shining!

And we smiled and I watched their backs leaving—
knowing no one else—she going back to Kansas and pain,
the unknown. She lingers so strongly in my heart.
Never did anything like that before—broke all the rules—
didn't even consider them for a moment.
She needed bread, to be fed, blessed, not go away so alone,
    unbefriended.

Then remembered how acutely I had wanted to just be alone,
undisturbed, when they walked into the row I was seated in.
I watched her take notes on a large, already used on one side,
sheet of paper. The word "Dad" was written at the top—her notes—
"Red day here" (it was Pentecost), ribbons, banners, candles.
I realized they were things she needed to keep—she wasn't really
listening to the readings—more to the soul of the words and singing.
We had smiled at one another while singing, not thinking twice—
We started sharing without words and I could hear the underlying
fear in her voice, trembling, shaking—the chemo, the cancer.
Was just visiting and going home tomorrow.
Dark hair, wide dark eyes in a round face—already lined with pain,
the shadow of mortality, being finite on the edge of infinity.
Bless her. Keep her child, her world. May she always have bread,
water, blessings, unknown friends so you can touch her tenderly.
May we all. Amen.

Vancouver Island,
British Columbia, Canada
1983–1984

IT WAS A LONG-TERM visit to do research for my thesis. The bishop was kind enough to allow me to work throughout the diocese. I was seeking to set up small base communities up and down the east side of the island—beginning in Victoria, up over the Malahat, to the northernmost end of the island and then into the Native reserves and back down again. I made the trip two or three times a week for more than four months.

When the research was done and it was almost time to return home I was feasted with a giveaway by some of the First Nations communities. I was going home loaded down with blankets striped in vibrant colors, mukluks beaded and furred, woven cloth, and a huge round bowl—with antelope, deer, and other creatures that ran around the outside— for making bread and mixing grains. There was a huge duffel bag filled with frozen slabs of salmon, halibut, and char steaks. And there was one large piece of soapstone, a sculpture, weathered green patina, weighing about eight pounds.

It was a woman sitting on the ice, fishing. She was bundled in clothes and boots, and hooded, her face surrounded with a halo of fur. Her hands, though, were bare, holding the line that ended in the open hole. Beside her there was a small pile of fish already caught. On her other side was a small dog stretched out the length of her extended legs, up against her, warming her.

I examined her closely. Exquisite strong simple lines, details carved into the stone: lines in her face, hair peeking out from her hood, crinkles around her eyes and lips. She was not a young woman. She was weathered with long living, caring, and surviving. It was the last gift given—with all of them standing around in a circle. They were careful to tell me this was a special gift from all of them. The green-grey patina shined—it had long been fingered and rubbed. It wasn't a newly sculpted piece—it was already seasoned and old. They began the presentation very formally but with twinkles in their eyes and before they could finish, a child blurted out, "It's supposed to be you! It's what you're really like—it's the way we see you." Much laughter and nodding heads responded.

I was startled. I bore no resemblance to this peace-filled, patient, seated woman fishing in the winter on ice! (Not that I could see.) I looked hard at it again, heavy yet fitting easily in my hands on my lap (I had been seated to receive the gifts). I noticed the hands—so strong, so delicately carved—and as I fingered the lines deep in the stone I became aware of something unexpectedly: each hand had a hole in it, a good-sized hole.

I asked, "Are the holes in her hands intended, or were they in the stone before the carving? They'd been patiently waiting (and hoping that I'd see them, I was told later). They all nodded solemnly.

"Yes," an elder, a woman spoke. "Everything is gift. The Great Spirit gives, sharing all that is made with us. All that we need is given: our food, what we wear, our tools, our homes—all comes to us through others. She—the woman receives the fish and it must pass through her hands (from God's) to others.

"You came to us asking if you could share the gospel so you could write your paper for school. We know it came to us as gift from the Spirit, so we gave you our words, our dreams and hopes, our struggles and questions, even some of our sorrows and pain. We gave you the truth of what we believe, what the Great Spirit has given to us. We shared with you—so we have exchanged gifts. You must remember: 'A gift is not a gift until you have given it at least twice!' It is even better if it is given more times and it moves around! All must pass through us. We have holes in our hands and in our hearts. You must always let it pass through you. This is our gift to you, now that you are one of us."

It was and is the best gift; they were the beginning of my vocation—not to preach the gospel to them or anyone but to draw forth (go fishing) the Word of God from others. Now I live remembering the holes made in our hands and hearts. Then there was much feasting, singing, and dancing to send me off.

Years ago, I gave her away. Part of me still wishes I hadn't parted with her, but I had to—the gift she symbolized had to be passed on to who needed it next. Our lives are really a continuous Giveaway.

Vestments and Glad Rags

I T WAS WINTER, COLD, wet, and a bit dreary as only Seattle and the Northwest can be in November. I had just flown into the airport that was crowded—close to Thanksgiving weekend. I'd come to do a series of talks and a parish mission since Advent would begin just a few days after the holiday. A couple from the parish had come to collect me, and we were heading to the parking structure with my bags. There was a huge elevator car, big enough to carry twenty to thirty people and some luggage carts too. The three of us were the only ones who got on, and up we started to the next levels. At the next floor we stopped and about twelve to fifteen people, not counting the children, got on with their carts. And we started again. I realized quickly that they were all one family—extended kin, but somehow all related. They were all chattering away, excited to see the ones just arriving, and they were bubbling over. And then there was an initial silence as they all got into the empty car and the three of us moved to the back to accommodate them, smiling at them all the while. Buttons were pushed and again we started up.

The talk picked up again. We spoke English. They spoke mostly Spanish, and within moments I recognized *Nautuhl* (the word means source, in the language of indigenous people of Guatamala). It is a distinct language, unique, unlike any other in the area, with guttural sounds; and yet it has tones that sing and rise and fall. We started stopping at every floor. Doors opened. The car was already packed full, so doors closed and we smiled at the people waiting to get on— and we went up again and laughed. The talk grew louder and louder. I realized they were looking sideways at me (not at the couple who picked me up and not straight on—that would be rude in their culture unless you're family). There were gestures; they were poking one another, with whispers, and then the comments grew louder, sounding like assertions, statements.

Then the door opened and the three of us in the back needed to get off. But instead of stepping aside so we could exit the car, they all got off and gathered around us. One of the two men who had been speaking both languages switched again and spoke to me in English. "Excuse me, please, but my family insists that I ask you; they have to know. Who are you? And why are you wearing a *huptil* (a native blouse) from their village in Guatemala?"

I had forgotten what I had on; I had come from another city where I had given a workshop and hadn't had time to change into my "traveling clothes." I had on one of my favorite blouses—a tunic of Guatemalan cotton made of various old scraps of cloth as well as a new piece that they'd been sewn onto. It was deep rich green; the design was flowered and rich with other colors, like the quetzal bird's feathers, and there was elaborate embroidery around the cuffs and neckline, and down the shoulders. I wore it often when I would speak in public. This blouse and other clothes I have been given I think of as my "glad rags," even vestments that I wear when I teach or preach.

I knew that each village in Guatemala had its own distinct patterns, weavings and designs that women wove on back strap looms, often handmade or strung between two trees. Just looking at the designs of these traditional pieces would reveal to anyone who was local/indigenous where you were from geographically and what clans and families you were bound to by birth and marriage. In many of the places where I traveled to do workshops and community organizing in churches, I would be given gifts—of cloth, of clothing, handcrafted, sometimes having been worn by two or three generations of the family for special occasions—old pieces sewn into newly woven ones. It was a high honor to both receive and give away one of these pieces. It was their way of saying I was one of them; I had been received into their family.

I smiled and in English and Spanish (I know only the sounds of Natuhl), I started to speak, and he began to translate line by line into both the other languages, to their rapt attention. I told him how I came to have this blouse. I had been teaching in Loyola of Chicago for many summers, and one of my students from Guatemala took a number of my classes. She wrote her papers in Spanish since she was still trying to learn English. After two summers, I became her advisor and then her thesis director, and her friend. After five summers, she was ready to graduate but she had no family in the country who could be invited to the ceremony, and it was customary for students to have parents or another family member to walk down the aisle with them to receive their diploma. She had approached me and asked if I would stand in for her family, and I was honored and delighted to. So it was arranged.

The day of the Mass and the giving of diplomas came, and just before we all lined up to file in with the procession, she gave me her gift of thanks that would bind me to her and proclaim me as one of her family: a blouse she had brought with her, and partially sewn herself. This huptil made of old and new—pieces that had been part of the ceremonial, celebratory clothes of her mother, grandmother, tias, and even great grandmother. Would I please wear it so they could be with her too? I put it on and we both walked in together, clothed in traditional Guatemalan dress. Afterward she said I must keep it, as I gave her a gift: an English/Spanish version of the Scriptures.

It had been at least six, maybe seven years since I had seen her (she moved to Canada to work with immigrant communities there), but I treasured her gift that tied me to her life, her family, her people and culture as well as her faith. I started to say her name—Maria (practically all names begin with Maria) Rosario Esperanza—and excitedly different voices piped up adding her other names. And I was introduced to and hugged and hugged by aunts, cousins, both men and women, and lastly, a bit shyly, a younger sister on her first visit to the States.

It was after midnight by now and we all had to continue on. They were visiting and would fly out in a few days, going to Vancouver, Canada, where they would meet up with her. We exchanged phone numbers, addresses (this was before email became the norm for communications), and after many blessings and wonder, they got back into the elevator and we went in search of the couples' car.

We were in Seattle, Washington. I had flown in from San Francisco (I live in New Mexico) and I had met their daughter/kin in

Chicago. They came in from Guatemala and were heading to Canada. The world had become small—in the universal kingdom of the Word made flesh and the Good News to the poor.

That night I realized how many gifts of cloth and how many handcrafted, lovingly made pieces of clothing were lasting ties to the people and families, believers and Christians I have had the privilege of being welcomed into as I visited them. I have been so blessed to stay with them, study the gospel with them, struggle for justice, and pray with them over the years. A piece I kept long until I passed it on to someone who "coveted it greatly" was a bright shocking-orange serape from a mountain mining community in Peru, made of baby-soft alpaca wool. Another was a deep Irish green-and-black-and-silver-fringed Apache dance shawl given to me so that I could dance in with the women elders of many nations at a huge congress. I was wrapped in it, loaned beaded deerskin moccasins, and long beaded earrings so that I could blend in with them, as we shuffled across Mother Earth (paved with concrete) in long, silent, moving rows to the drum's beat.

There have been prayer shawls, ruanas, serapes, bolts of cloth, silk (Thailand, Myanmar), sashes/old obis and short kimonos from Japan, also crafted of old elegant fabrics and new silks; scarves (Singapore, New Zealand) and ones made of feathers (from Australia, Malaysia), leis of flowers, fresh when I would arrive in Hawaii and the Marshall Islands and dried ones when I left, made from all sorts of grasses. There are mats woven tightly from island bushes and rugs that grace my floors and walls, mostly old, parted with as signs of living together still and bags (to carry coca leaves to chew on and help me breathe and steady my heart at high altitudes) and to travel on short trips unexpectedly. Another I wear often is South African cloth, fashioned into a long skirt, tunic and hat in the shape of a drum, head coverings. I wear them, minus the hat that would make me about a foot taller than I actually am! A few I wear when I speak in public—my signature along with dangling earrings from the Lakotas and other tribes, scarves from Ireland and a Sundance blanket. I wrap them around me for warmth and sometimes use them as a security blanket (a la Peanuts) and to pray in at night alone (as I go behind my blanket, as the Native peoples say, but still stay connected to the larger community). They are cherished and are part of my identity that proclaims I am kin to them, I live in solidarity with them, and I am, with them, a citizen of the Kingdom of God. I am often teased, and sometimes told seriously that I always wear the same clothes; why don't I get some new ones? It's too much to explain. I smile and say I'm attached to them because of who gave them to me.

I will always remember a Mass and burial in Nicaragua for a catechist who had been "disappeared," the body left in pieces along the side of a road, lovingly collected and buried with "honors." When the liturgy and shared remembrances were over, the altar was stripped except for the catechist's serape that had served as an altar cloth. Everyone sat very still. I was quietly told that whoever would go up to the altar and pick up the serape, and put it over their shoulders would be the one to take the place and continue the ministry the catechist had fulfilled in giving their life for the preaching of the gospel. It had become the ritual. The serape, often stained with blood and sometimes with the wine of the Mass, would become the stole of the one who would take the risk and dare to take up the preaching of the Good News to the poor. It was done in silence. The person wrapped the vestment around the shoulders and over the head and led the people out to live the Word in the world.

This passing on of tradition, of preaching the Word of God fearlessly, faithfully in hard times and with joy has a long history in our faith. It is shared in the mantle of the prophets such as Elijah, who drops his cloak so that Elisha can snatch it up and bear a double portion of Spirit to speak on behalf of the poor, the forgotten of God. The prophet declares the honor of God, what constitutes true worship, and the imperative of doing justice and caring for the poor. This is the background that Jesus invokes, on the night he leaves earth rising and blessing his friends from a hill outside Jerusalem, as he tells them: "Remain in the city and wait until you are clothed with power from on high, for I will give you the gift of the Father— my own Spirit" (cf. Luke 24:49).

All these tangible gifts tie me strongly to the people, places, and struggles for justice; to the poor preaching the gospel, the communities of hope—those who have converted me, made me more human, compassionate, and true, even more daring. It is all of them who have taught me how to live as a disciple of Jesus, the poor one, the Son of Man, the Son of Justice, the Son of the living God. I originally thought I was going to be a missionary and preach the Good News to the poor, but it is they who have preached to me. It is they who are the Good News, the Word taking on flesh today who have drawn me into the community of Church; who have been saving me all along. They have initiated me into God's dwelling place on earth and wrapped me in its embrace of hope. They have shared with me the power and authority of the poor, living the Word, stronger than any education, degree, professional experience, even ordination. They are all my kin—my family bound by the blood of the cross, the wine of rejoicing in the resurrection and the mantle of the Word.

And I remember often, what so many said to me as I was leaving, especially in Central and South America: "Go home, gringa—it's your people who need the gospel. Preach to your own—it's harder! And don't worry, we won't forget you! Just make sure when you die or at least when they bury you, you're wearing our clothes. Then when you get to the doors of heaven, if you have trouble getting in—we'll tell them: Look! See! She's really one of us—see, she's wearing our clothes (they are garments given like baptismal robes). And if they are still undecided about letting you in—don't worry. At night, go round back and we'll throw a rope ladder over the wall and pull you up and in!

I give many of these gifts away when people admire them (a custom in many Latin American countries: you compliment it—it's yours!) but I keep a few, just in case I need to use my "glad rags, my vestments of the poor," to get me in and home forever.

"You Are My Child, This Day I Have Begotten You."

THERE WERE A GOOD number of us—twice as many girls as boys in the family. We were pushed to excel at anything we tried. So, there was a good deal of constant competition. We all wanted approval, especially from our father—though it was rarely given—at least not outright. Usually approval was given in half-compliments, in comparison to someone else. My father had a saying that we all (almost outwardly) groaned when he would say it to one of us. "You know", he'd say, "you're one of my favorite daughters. You're one of my favorite sons." He didn't want to play favorites (though of course we all knew who actually already was in that place). But he thought it was enough, and that it kept the peace among us all.

My friend has been a missionary in South Florida for more than half a century. Originally he's from the rough, western coast of Ireland, but he was recruited when most of the state was still designated as mission territory, up until the 1960s. He was stationed in a range of parishes, but he also worked full time with the Haitians, the Blacks, the Salvadorans, and the Guatemalans; many of whom worked in the cane fields and on huge farms. They lived in squalor and misery. Most were illegal; most were men far from their families trying to earn money to send home. Conditions were appalling—indentured slavery wasn't far from their lived reality.

He'd often go to their home countries, to connect with family. Over the years he had been made legal guardian to many children whose fathers had died in canals and accidents while working under brutal, dangerous, and illegal conditions. He had a small cadre of lawyers working with him to get them their rights and to disperse the monies that were court-appointed after many public trials.

On one trip to Haiti he was walking from one small village to another, looking for a family. He followed various sets of directions and found himself on a fairly deserted unpaved road, hot, dry, and dusty in a rural area. Ahead he could see a woman walking toward him: a basket on her head and a baby maybe a year or two old on her hip. My friend spoke Creole and some French (along with other languages) and planned to greet her when she came closer to him. But, distracted for a moment, he was looking across the fields on either side of the road. When he looked again, she'd left the road and was heading across the field, through turned, ragged rows. He looked around; there were no real paths and no houses or shacks anywhere in sight. He worried if she left the road to avoid him: a white man and she being alone. Then as he watched her, about thirty yards into the field she disappeared, and he realized that she must have sat down.

As he approached her, he spoke and greeted her and she responded. He headed into the field and they made small talk. The child was sitting on the ground playing in the dirt. He sat down too. She was rolling small mounds of dirt in her long, tapering fingers. She spit using her saliva so that she formed small balls of mud. And she was slowly eating them—a number of them lined up beside her neatly in the dirt. She would roll them around in her mouth, softening it and swallow it in pieces. He didn't know what to say. He'd heard of people being so hungry that they ate dirt but hadn't really believed it—until now.

They talked. He asked directions and she indicated that he wasn't far; to keep going in the same direction and he'd soon see the houses. And then she continued, explaining to him why she was sitting a ways off the road, in the field. "It's the dirt," she said. She was pregnant and she had to eat, but she had to think of her child so she only ate good dirt there in the field, away from the road where people walked and where the dirt was foul and dirty. That's why she was there. Eventually he helped her up, blessed her (by this time he'd told her who he was), and they both went back to the road together. They both continued on their way, waving as they parted.

When he told me this story, I was appalled; but then the next time I was in Haiti, just months later—on the far western coast of the island, in a small village looking out into the vast water—I was in the marketplace looking for food. I saw this stacked bunch of oval lumps of what looked like mud. I asked. They were made of dirt laced with sugar or other things like cinnamon and pieces of herbs that were local, and they were for sale. So many people were eating dirt that some of the women tried to make it more palatable and added to it, trying to make a small profit. I bought a couple and ate one. It was filling. It was gross and definitely mostly dirt. (I wondered where the dirt came from; was it good dirt or really foul dirt?)

I have not been able to forget the story and the reality it belies, but what struck me the most was the woman's concern for her unborn, developing child. She had to eat, but the dirt had to be the cleanest she could find—off the beaten path like in the middle of a field. Her child yet to be born was so loved, as much as, if not more than her own life.

(For Frank)

PART II

It was in the 1980s in El Salvador during the heavy fighting that raged throughout the country, often worse in the small villages far from the cities, in the mountains and off the main roads. The people were caught between government troops and the rebel forces. They were often visited by the rebels coming down from their hideouts higher up, who took food, clothing, tools, and often the younger ones, especially the boys, back with them, tearing apart families. And then the military would arrive, accusing the villagers of collaborating with the guerillas, and take more of what little was left to the people, brutalizing, raping, wantonly killing, and taking any of the younger ones who were still there.

I was visiting with catechists and had been in the village for almost a week with a team, teaching, praying, doing the gospel, singing, and working with them. They cared for me and the other team members, sharing graciously of what they had. We were getting ready to move on to the next village. A truck would collect us in the morning and we were celebrating Mass, to be followed by a small fiesta. And then word came that there was a contingent of soldiers en route, headed straight for the village. They had been "visited" before and the elders met immediately. Within minutes it was decided that everyone would leave right then and there. They were ready. Everyone took what they could carry on their backs, and they started walking into the foothills and heavy brush. There were men, not many, women—mostly carrying children, and the old ones, everyone helping each other two by two or in threes. In a long, long line they spread out, and they were silent. We went with them. We had heard of the massacres, the rapes, and the soldiers burning everything when they didn't find what or who they were looking for—there was no reasoning with them.

We walked for hours, handing children around as people tired. The dark came, a night with no moon, good for us. Finally, the leaders called a halt. We'd rest on the trail, spread out in groups of ten or twelve until the hours just before dawn. There were to be no fires, no talking except as absolutely necessary, and everyone was to try to keep the children quiet and hopefully get some sleep, or at least rest. We settled down and rolled up next to each other for warmth but more for a sense of another body next to our own, rocking the children and trying to sleep. An hour or two later, word came that a group of soldiers were not far—in fact they were parallel to the long line of the villagers. They were only a couple of hundred yards away through the underbrush that was thick. Silence had to be maintained. It was literally a question of life or death for everyone.

A young woman who was very pregnant was with us. She had had great difficulty walking and breathing and was already in the beginning stages of labor when we'd left hours before. Now her labor had started in earnest, speeded up by the walking. No matter what was happening around us, she was going to give birth—the child could not be held back.

She moved away from the elders and children, and a number of women gathered, forming a cocoon around her and holding her—her head, shoulders, arms, and hands, underneath her and holding her legs. I was with them, one of her hands tightly gripping my own. She kept quiet, trying to control her breathing and panting, let alone any sound that would escape her. She squeezed hands and dug her nails into the skin of the women holding her. We were all breathing with her. A woman put a thick twig in her mouth to bite down on and covered her mouth with a cloth. And for hours she labored—in total silence. It was as though we all labored. She willed. She pushed, collapsed, and gathered her strength again. She sweated and not a sound came from her.

Hours later as the light was just starting (it had been decided no one would move until the child was born) I was watching her face, drenched in sweat, her lips bloodied from biting them and her tongue, her eyes wide. And then the last final push and the child slipped out, born into this world, caught by deft hands; the umbilical cord was cut and the little body wrapped. She was shining, wiped out, dried off, somewhat cleaned, and held strongly. They stroked her with their hands, their faces, their cheeks next to hers. It was as though time stopped. And then we all stood up together. Still no one spoke. It was utterly still. She was raised up; the word traveling to the front with a gesture of rocking a baby! Everyone fell into line and the walk began again. There were arms around her, another held her baby. Two held her between them, three across, their arms over her shoulders and around her waist, in step with one another.

We walked for another couple of hours and came to a small cluster of houses. We were welcomed. The soldiers had veered off in the night. Everyone was safe for now. Food was shared around and slowly people began to talk again. First in whispers; then the children started piping up, louder.

I sat with the women. We started to smile and laugh, the tension and tightness we carried easing out of our bodies. We even started sharing scratches and nail marks on our hands, arms, and faces where the young woman had clutched at us and dug into us. And we were crying. After a while I crept over toward her. She was resting and nursing her newborn, her firstborn. We looked at each other and

I asked, "Please may I ask you a question?" She beamed at me and nodded. "How did you do it? How did you stifle all sound, say nothing and not cry out? All those hours?" Others were listening now.

She waited a moment and then spoke. "I had to. My child had to be born. You see—my child might be 'El Salvador'—the one we are all waiting for—the child that will bring peace to us all." Looking down at the baby wrapped in her arms and heart, she continued, "She might be 'El Salvador.'" The others nodded. I was silenced. She handed me her child to hold. I looked into the tiny, wrinkled face—this child—her only child; what child is this?

Weeks later, I thought again of this newborn and I remembered my father's words said so often to each of us: "You know, you're one of my favorite daughters; one of my favorite sons." And I knew I had been given wisdom by these women. On that walk and during that birth I learned that God, El Salvador, loves each one of us—each of his beloved children—as though we are an only child. He loves each of us as he loves his only begotten Son, his firstborn among us, Jesus. God loves us, each as an only child, and who knows who each of us is born to be? God knows. We are meant to give birth to one another, to call one another forth because we are all loved as his only child and we are born to communion with Jesus, the Father, and their Spirit. One of God's favorite daughters...one of God's favorite sons!

Child's Play:
Redeeming the Moment

I T HAD BEEN A hard week, the week before the war in Iraq, the second one, started. It was the second week of Lent—a Lent without any reflection, penance, or conversion. The readings were clear about who is God! It began with the story of Abraham being told point-blank not to do anything to harm his child. God wanted his obedience not blood sacrifice. It is a benchmark in human and Jewish history. God does not want our children, or our enemies' children, or anyone's life. God wants worship, humility, a sense of right relationship, and awe. And then in the gospel there is the story of what we call the Transfiguration: Jesus with Moses and Elijah on either side of him, turned toward him as the center of the universe—and his future passage in Jerusalem on the cross. Moses who is the liberator, the lawgiver, and the strongest of the prophets with Elijah, "the disturber of Israel," turned in respect to listen to Jesus.

The tension in the Church was palatable. And then came the overshadowing of the mountain and disciples with the cloud of Exodus and the fear it invoked. Then the voice that cried out: "This is my Beloved Child, my Beloved Son. Listen to him!" (cf. Luke 9:35). And when they looked up there was only Jesus.

I recently had been driving down the Florida Turnpike and had seen a sign that reminded me of Moses and the Ten Commandments. It read, in stark white on black: "WAR? Not in My Name, not now, not ever! God." And in parenthesis: "(What piece of "Thou Shalt Not' do you not understand?)" This came to mind now as I sat in that church.

"This is my Beloved Child, my Beloved Son. Listen to him!" Those were the words that began to evoke hostility and anger. One could feel it rising from rows of pews. "Listen to Him. Listen to the Word of the Lord. Listen to the Scriptures." Jesus had been preaching about how hard it would be to be his disciples in the world, "to deny ourselves, pick up our cross and come after him." Deny ourselves, so that we don't deny him. "Love your enemies, pray for those who hate you. Bless those who curse you. Do good to those who harm you" (Luke 6:27–28). And the disciples weren't listening. Instead they were listening to their own fears, and their hopes for a place in the sun, hopes for nationalism and the overthrowing of the Romans, of vindication. They were listening to the murmur that was rising around them, of hate, of disagreement, of blasphemy.

They are just like us. Who are we listening to as our country proclaims that it is going to war unprovoked, unilaterally, in a pre-emptive strike, though every religious leader, including our own? John Paul II said that this is wrong, a disaster for humans and a tragedy for religious people.

That's when they started getting up and leaving, crawling over people, slamming doors, huffing and puffing down the main aisle, muttering as they went.

Listen! Listen to my beloved! And there was only Jesus there—and nationalism, other religions besides the God of Jesus, the Crucified One. The last night of the parish mission, it was over.... As I walked out of the church, someone came up to me and with glee said, "It's started! They bombed Iraq tonight!" I nearly cried, and said, "God have mercy on us all."

Outside in the church vestibule there were a lot of people, talking about the news, buying books, having coffee and continuations of the earlier discussions. People were getting loud and angry, gesturing, then accusing and even cursing. I was surrounded by people and then a young girl approached me—maybe nine or ten years old, and she had a handful of bumper stickers with her. She interrupted everyone and asked me if I'd take one of her bumper stickers and put it on my car. I was trapped! I asked her what it said and she told me, "no," she wouldn't tell me, only that it was what Jesus would want us to do.

The two of us looked at each other and I took a wild risk: "OK, I'll take one of your bumper stickers and put it on my car, as soon as I get back home." She solemnly handed it to me, and, as I read it, I did cry. It said: "JESUS SAYS LOVE YOUR ENEMIES. I think that means don't kill them." I was stunned, and I asked her for about twenty more, which she gave me with a big grin on her face.

Her father, who was standing behind her, wasn't pleased, and she turned to him and said, "See, I told you she'd know it was true." I asked her where she found these and she informed me that she used her allowance that she earned to have them made—a couple of hundred of them. I looked at her father and said, "Your daughter is a blessing and wise in the ways of love already. She has redeemed this moment of despair, anger and war. I am grateful for your daughter's words and courage." And he cried. Others did not and just left, silenced for the moment.

Redeeming the moments. Redeeming the times. Redeeming graces. That is what all of us must be about every day, everywhere. We are believers in the resurrection and we are called to practice it now! No matter what—harm, hate, isolation, arrogance, self-righteousness, stupidity—we are to redeem it all, one moment, one situation, one person, one nation, one historical reality at a time. It has to be done with the courage of a child, telling the truth in the midst of emotion and lies, reminding us of the essentials and the obvious, interrupting the discussions and simply stating it—irrefutably.

Arundhati Roy, speaking at the World Social Forum at Porto Alegre, Brazil, on January 27, 2003, said it in her direct and passionate words:

> ...Our strategy should be not only to confront empire, but to lay siege to it. To deprive it of oxygen. To shame it. To mock it. With our art, our music, our literature, our stubbornness, our joy, our brilliance, our sheer relentlessness, and our ability to tell our own stories. Stories that are different than the ones we're being brainwashed to believe.
>
> The corporate revolution will collapse if we refuse to buy what they are selling—their ideas,

their version of history, their wars, their weapons, their notion of inevitability. Remember this: We be many and they be few. They need us more than we need them.

Another world is possible, she is on her way. On a quiet day, I can hear her breathing." (This is a woman who has called for the globalization of compassion.)

We are called to redeem our portion of the universe, our piece of time with our grace and truth, and the Word of God made flesh among us still. We are called to witness to Jesus' kingdom, to Jesus' conspiracy of compassion and life of making enemies into dear friends. This day I call upon all of us to practice the fine art of redemption. May Grace prevail upon us. Amen.

Discernment

WHEN I FIRST MOVED to New Mexico more than thirty years ago, I did a good deal of work on some of the fifteen-plus pueblos (the word means "the people" and was the word used to describe Native American reservations in this part of the Southwest through the long history of conquest by the Spain). But before I actually did any work on the pueblos, I was taken to be introduced to them by one of my students.

She had an apartment in town but had her house on the Pueblo land. Property and houses were passed on from mother to youngest daughter (among many Native peoples, you are native through your mother's bloodline). She was well respected among her people and had studied to be a drug/alcohol abuse counselor and served as a liaison between the people who lived on Indian land; those who came and went and the various organizations and services that worked with the Native peoples in regard to health, welfare, education, and human services. Her pueblo was Jemez, one of the larger ones, but also one that was "off the beaten path"—not on the list of tourist sites.

I was taken over a period of a couple of months as her friend and teacher to feast-day celebrations that began with Mass, followed by dances, open to the public for viewing, and gatherings of families that continued more privately inside the adobe dwellings, while the tourists stayed in more public areas around the plaza. I was warned: at each house you will be fed: posole, stew, fresh corn, beans, squash, tortillas, sweet breads, juice, fry bread—all manner of food and delicacies that are part of each family's traditions. You have to eat at every house, so take a little of this and a little of that—of everything. But pace yourself because we'll be visiting ten or twelve different houses and clans. She spoke with knowledge. At each place I was welcomed warmly, introduced to the elders first and was taken to meet each person in the house, and plates of food would appear—served usually by children, but they could be handed to me by just about anyone. I learned to nibble and keep fry bread at hand in case something was especially hot—red or green chile and spices.

Then one weekend I went to a celebration, attended church and sang with the Indian choir, followed by the dances, and then was brought to a house and taken into the kitchen. All the women and most of the children were in one half of the house and the men in the other half: the walls had been removed so that it was just two long rooms. My friend reintroduced me to some of the women and said she had to go and see someone, one of her aunties, and she'd be back in a couple of hours. And she was gone.

I felt awkward, not knowing anyone. I was seated toward the end of a long table. Around me everyone was cooking, chopping, dicing, peeling: they all seemed to have their jobs as they turned out heaping platters of food, pots of beans, flipping stacks of tortillas and rolling dough for fry bread. The place steamed and smelled of all the food cooking. Then a woman came up to me with a child, around two or three years old from the size of him, and she put him in my lap, smiled at me and asked, "Can you take care of him and keep him out of the way—and away from the stove and oven—or anything he can get into and especially off the floor?" I was relieved.

"Sure!" and I lifted him around to face me.

Morris West called this child, in one of his novels, one of the "clowns of God."

He was autistic. I realized he was probably more like six years old, not as young as I originally thought, just severely physically underdeveloped for his age. For the next forty-five to fifty minutes, he climbed all over me. He played with my clothes, my face—exploring, poking, looking intently at every piece of me that he could get near, making all sorts of noises and grunts. Then he started on my hair (it has long been white, since my late twenties, and long.)

I have worked with many native people, and in many areas of the world, one's hair is important. It has to be long—the longer the better because your hair is your tie to your ancestors, reflecting the long tradition of wisdom. Short, cropped hair means no ties, no wisdom, nothing worth listening to. And white hair is even better! It singles you out as touched by the Great Spirit.

Among the women around me in the kitchen that day, all wore their hair tied up in ritual knots for ceremonies and dances. The men wore theirs down, long. Then, if necessary, the Great Spirit could seize hold of one of them by his hair and pull him up to question him on behalf of the people.

I wore mine piled up and wrapped around the back of my head, held in place by clips and combs, to keep it off my face. In no time at all the boy was intent on pulling out long white strands—removing them piece by piece from their carefully tied up and twisted place. He chewed on my hair, sucked on it, and pulled it. Soon my hair was completely a mess and all of it down and hanging. He'd twist it around his fingers. Then he started squirming and wanting to get down. So we started light tickling, making noises, humming, pulling faces as I tried to keep him somewhat content to stay on my lap or draped heavily over my shoulder.

And then, out of nowhere he lurched and threw up all over me and he was thoroughly delighted with himself and the mess, playing with it and smearing it over me and himself. At this point all I could do was laugh (or else I'd cry). No one seemed to be paying any attention to us at all. We were in our own little world. Eventually I got up and I carried him over to a sink so I could try to clean us both up a bit. It didn't help much but the first wet layer of crap was removed. And then back we went to the end of the long table. I grabbed some of the fry bread (each pueblo has its own style) and began tearing off little pieces, making stick figures and lining them up on the table, like dolls. We'd play with them and then eat them. I'd feed him and he'd feed me and then he was suddenly interested in teeth, mouth, tongue, and eyes again.

Again I looked around. It had grown a bit quiet, the pace of preparation had slowed, and one by one the women came and sat at the table bringing coffee and tea cups, canned milk and sugar. One of the older women came and took the child I'd been entrusted with from me, and he was passed from woman to woman and then taken to another part of the house. I was given a cup of coffee and a wet rag. As I cleaned my face, one of the women took down my hair, now matted with stuff and snarled. I probably looked, as my nana would say: like a banshee (Irish version of cuandera/good witch) with wild white hair. With deft movement she combed it out, did a few twists, and piled it up in place with a beaded hairclip, the way they wore their hair. It had grown silent while she did my hair.

Then my friend appeared and joined us at the table. She hadn't ever left. It was a ruse to leave me alone. If I was to be a teacher, an elder (in spite of my age, I was only in my forties) among them, I had to be seen and tested by them. And the little boy was the one who decided for them whether or not I was to be accepted, unbeknownst to me. And thank God I'd passed the test. They had all been watching how one young child and I got on—whether or not he would, first of all, just stay with me and if I was patient and careful of him, treating him with respect no matter what he did.

They believed that their "special needs children," as they are often referred to now, are gifts of the Spirit, and they see them as ones who can see through people almost instantly, "truth-tellers of another's intentions and spirit." They know they can read people on many levels that aren't immediately apparent or perceived by others, especially adults. It is the authority, the power of the child who sees like the Great Spirit sees. They told me that the deciding factor for many of them was when he started taking my hair down and I let him (he was very insistent and persistent!) and that when he threw up all over me I didn't yell at him or chastise him at all, and still kept holding him.

They all smiled, and plates of food appeared, and I was told I would be welcome to come and teach on the pueblo, that everyone would come; that the word was already going round the houses. They asked if I would teach the same classes and things that I did in the other churches and parishes of the diocese. I told them: of course, or I'd teach them whatever they'd like me to teach. They already knew, from my friend, what I taught—the Scriptures and stories and how I taught: going back and forth with them, pulling what they thought out of them, pushing them to find words for what they knew. My initiation rite was over. We could begin to study the Scriptures together, and I could begin to learn their ways and beliefs. They would share what they believed and trust me. And one of them said, "We can start right now. You can tell us some stories—one of Jesus' and one about the earth or from your people." So we began right then and there using the gospel from early that morning at the celebration and then a story about creation and how the Great Spirit is still creating today.

This pattern of stories of Jesus from the Scriptures and traditional tales from other peoples' history and culture and others from around the world became the way I taught in all the places I visited. And I was the one who would come home the richer, the wiser by far because they shared their stories and acquired wisdom with me. There is a saying among storytellers worldwide: "There is only one story to tell. How do you tell it?" Over the years, all I have taught and written has been gleaned and harvested from the wisdom, stories, history, experience, and lived faith that has been shared with me by so many others. Others have taught me that "All stories are true, some of them actually happened; and when I say 'Once upon a time,' this one is going to happen to you, now."

Religion is perhaps this: to make the stories of God come true today in us, as Jesus the Word made Flesh dwelling among us continues the Good News to the poor in our flesh and histories together. The end story, still being told, is the Trinity, communion of all peoples in our God.

Remembering

Her old face collected and dispersed light
like a thin gossamer butterfly wing or a sea-washed shell.
She possessed her own specific radiance unselfconsciously.
Isolated in dementia, her memories blurring childhood and age.
In the beginning we were formed of such translucent clay.
In the end perhaps we die this way, utterly penetrated by Light.

Eighty-two years old she embodied reverence or transcendence.
She was four feet, ten. Her eyes blue liquid washes
shimmering in her porcelain face.
Her form so emaciated her bones shone through.
I was afraid she'd break as I turned her from the wall.
She was heavy as silk, her veins delicate white lines
in the fabric falling through my fingers.
I held her as she died, the light slowly stealing away
going out like dusk settling around me.
All I can think of now was the play of light in medieval cathedrals.
She was the purest person I ever drew near. I pray something
of her glory lingers in me still, like fire buried in a cave.

*(Visiting the indigenous dying in Holy Cross Hospital, the Bronx, NY, the winter I
moved there. She'd come in off the street; only was there a couple of weeks. 1969.)*

Mary, Shadow of Grace

THERE IS A STORY that tells who Mary might be in the world today and what the world might be at its heart. It is a hard story, full of images, like the vision of John in Revelation.

It happened in 1976 in Chiapas, Mexico. I had been invited to a refugee camp to visit with some of the people who worked there. The refugees were Guatemalan Indians in exile, tired and beaten but still proud and dignified, waiting to go home, yet trying to build a small area where they could live in the meantime. The camps were huge, seventy or eighty miles inside the Mexican border, and the Church was their protector from the soldiers.

I arrived in July, and it was hot and muggy. There was one water spigot for forty thousand people, and it was a good long walk and a longer wait to get two buckets of water. In the family I stayed with, as with others, much of the talk revolved around who was going to get the water that day. Going was hard, but coming back was harder because of the temptation to drink the water

I had been there a few days, and my shoes had disappeared, brand new Reeboks. I had been given another pair, a spare pair, but they didn't fit well. They were too tight, had no laces, and were already well worn. But shoes are shoes.

My turn at the water spigot came every three or four days. So, my turn came again, and off I went. By the time I got there, my feet were raw and blistered. I was limping. When I got to the line waiting for a turn at the spigot, my biggest question was whether to take off the shoes and let my feet rest awhile or just moan and groan and try to ignore my screaming feet. There were sixty or seventy waiting in line, and it moved slowly. Most of the women didn't speak Spanish; they were more at ease in their own native tongues. I spoke a little

Spanish; together we probably knew about the same amount. So we didn't talk much.

This day, and each time I went to get the water, there was one woman who interrupted the line and changed the atmosphere totally. She was very tiny, about four feet, five inches, and dressed in black from head to toe. I thought how incredibly hot she must be. She would come up to the line, and all the conversations would stop abruptly. Everybody would move out of the way and let her go to the tap and get her water. She would very slowly fill up her one bucket and then leave. There was absolute silence while she was around. Nothing was said to her or about her.

I was intrigued and began to ask around about her. The only answer I got was—she's a little crazy, out of it. She thinks she's the Virgin Mary, la Madre. I wondered if she was the one by the church most days. There was a small adobe church and a large cross out in front.

This woman would lean up against the cross for hours without end, just standing there. No one seemed to know where she lived, but they knew that all her children and her husband were dead, brutally murdered, and all her sisters and brothers had disappeared or been tortured to death.

They would say, sadly, "She thinks she's the Virgin. She goes every day and stands at the foot of the cross and thinks that Jesus is being killed. Everyone treats her with respect and leaves her in her grief, but she's touched."

The day my feet were bleeding, I was about twenty people away from the water tap when the woman in black came. Everyone moved aside to let her in, and she filled her bucket. There was silence. But this time she didn't go away. This time she walked down the line and stopped right in front of me. I was nervous. I will never forget her face. She had an old, old face, but her eyes were bright, full of fire. She looked at me, and then she bent down and poured precious water on my feet and started washing my feet with the bottom part of her dress. She patted my feet dry and dug some muslin out of her pockets. She wrapped my feet with great care and then helped me put my shoes back on. Then she stood up in front of me, almost smiled, and said very quietly, "Ve con Dios, mi hija"—"Go with God, my daughter." Then she went back down the line, filled her bucket again, and left.

The silence after she had gone was much longer this time. Then one of the older women put her arm around me and repeated the other woman's greeting, "Ve con Dios, mi hija." From then on, everyone spoke to me, even if I didn't understand their language, and they brought me small gifts of food and cloth. I was accepted.

I don't think the old woman was "touched." I think she was the Virgin. Everywhere I go, I wonder where she is today. She is always in the place where there is welcome and tender regard even in the midst of horror. There is a certain amount of reverence toward her, but nobody really knows her. Maybe people think she's a little bit "touched."

Perhaps we all need to be a little bit "touched" that way. The woman still lives in the desert and has the wings of the eagle and eyes of fire. She has soft, healing balm, especially for the poor, those in pain, and those who are outsiders.

Wisdom Plays
before the Lord

I T WAS A FARM worker parish, in the late 1970s, north of Sacramento, California. It was already hot, dry, dusty, windy, late in Lent. I came to do a parish mission, in Spanish and English. It was a huge parish. The pastor welcomed me when I drove up from San Francisco. He said it was the first time they'd had a woman do a mission, and an Anglo too. The first Mass would be in a couple of hours—Saturday night and it would be very crowded, as all the Masses would be.

I was nervous about my Spanish, but I'd only been doing parish missions for a couple of years. They were usually in Lent on the long scriptures of John's gospel. I told the gospels by heart instead of reading them. I was assured practically everyone was fluent in English and not to be concerned.

The the pastor seemed a little nervous. I asked, "Is there anything else I need to know?

He hemmed and hawed a bit and then he said, "You probably should know that there will be music, a lot of it—and there will be an old woman who attends. Nobody really knows how old she is, but probably in her mid- to late-nineties. She has a cane that she leans on; she calls it her third leg. She'll be listening to you with great care. Sometime after you finish preaching, she'll approach you and everyone will be watching and waiting to see how she greets you and responds to your words."

I had the sense there was more to what he was saying. I asked, "Yes?"

His response: "She's been in the parish since before it was a parish. She came in the first wave of farm workers more than sixty years ago. She did the classes for adults and children for all the sacraments and preparation; Bible studies, working with families for baptisms and with the young people, even preparing people for marriage. She knows everyone's story, and everyone knows her and they go to her with their problems. She even seeks them out if she senses there are issues or something needs to be handled. She's probably La Madre (godmother) to more than half the parish, through two or three generations.

"She will come up to you, either as soon as you finish, or at the kiss of peace, or at the end of Mass. She's a small woman but very sharp and spry, full of energy, and feisty. If she welcomes you then everyone will come to the mission."

Now I was really nervous and edgy. I had worked in enough Hispanic communities to know she was the curandera, and she had at least as much respect and power among the people as the pastor, if not more. I knew that how she greeted me would be a make-or-break point. She was the oldest elder of the community. I was already sweating in the heat. Now I was praying passionately that the Word would be heard and that the Spirit would come singing and shining through me (that I wouldn't get in the way) and that they would be open and receptive. It was trust time.

I preached, after proclaiming the gospel by heart. I don't remember what I said. I told a story and asked them a question about the reading and suggested that they share what the Spirit had stirred in them with whoever was sitting next to them. There was a moment of silence and then they started talking. Then it was how to pull them back? Eventually I asked the question again and had a few people share their insights or what they heard from who they spoke with—in English and in Spanish. Then I finished preaching, wrapping things up and pulling together a few of their statements, ending with a story, and led back into the liturgy. I went and sat down at the end of the first row of chairs. I realized I was shaking (which was good. I knew the shakes said I wasn't taking the Word or preaching for granted. The Spirit shakes us up a little).

They started up the music, which was strong and lively, with everyone singing—they were used to singing together, and I slowly calmed down. The offertory gifts were brought up by families and lines of people brought food to share with those who needed it afterward. Then liturgy unfolded, up to the kiss of peace. The passing of the peace took a good long while, hugs, kisses, abrazos, laughing (and singing too). They greeting me and graciously drew me in. The music continued. And then I saw her: white haired, her head wrapped in braids, long skirt. She was weathered, wrinkled, eyes bright, coming toward me with her cane. Everyone deferred to her and bowed, reverently, warmly, and lovingly.

She stood in front of me for a moment, and we looked at one another. I didn't know exactly what to do—to kiss her cheek or her hands. She was the one who moved and I was taken aback, absolutely stunned. She slowly knelt down in front of me and kissed my feet (I had sandals on) and kept murmuring quietly, like praying: "Blessed are the feet of she who brings good news."

I bent over, pulling her up to her feet, crying and saying, "Please, please." And we held each other, then kissed each other with the words of the peace of Christ, paz de Christo. I was nearly paralyzed. The "Agnus Dei" continued, and she stood beside me, holding my hand, like a grandmother with her grandchild. When it was time for communion, we went hand in hand together. The priest handed her the bread. She smiled and broke hers in half and gave the other piece to me. And then she led me back to where I had been sitting and we sat side by side until the end of Mass.

When the closing hymn began, she took me by the hand again and we walked out behind the servers with the priest—out the door and over to the tables that had been set up under the trees, laden with food. It was their custom to share the evening meal. Then she took me around and introduced me to each family, groups of young people, others who looked as old as she did.

That evening, many hours later, in a borrowed bed in a back room, I thought about her. She was La Pastora, and thankfully, the designated pastor/priest knew that and honored her. She had been the apostle founding the church; the disciple/teacher and preacher for all these years. I was overjoyed that she had loved the gospel—the Good News to the poor—and was that Good News herself, incarnating the words in her flesh and life. And I was so grateful that she had been so gracious to me, blessing me with her acceptance, like

Elizabeth with Mary, validating my faith, confirming me in believing the announcement of the Incarnation. She was the living tradition of the people.

From that night on, I knew that I was called to preach the gospel, in season and out and to proclaim the Scriptures, telling them with my heart, looking at people and summoning them to hear, face to face—whenever, wherever I could—as she had done with her whole life of faithfulness in service to her community, family and friends.

Later that evening I heard her name spoken lovingly. Sophia. Of course, she embodied the wisdom of the community and helped them all to play in the presence of the Lord. She was the sermon I have never forgotten. It was probably the strongest preaching of the wisdom of the Word that only the poor know and can share with us. I began to learn that if I was to preach the Good News to the poor, then I must be one of them, and seek to be a friend of God, by being friends with them. The poor are the doorway into the deepest recesses of God's heart. Among them we begin to know our poor God, the Trinity, holy together. Sophia welcomed me home.

Snow, the Child

It snowed all night, frigid, cold.
But early the sun came out dancing glittering stars
beckoning sledders and snow boarders.
A hill in front of me—good sized one.
A small boy maybe five appeared at the top
sat, tucked his snowsuit in around him.
No sled but gave himself a push and slid—skimming—on the icy
covering of snow.
Pure delight and pleasure radiating from him, a smile so broad!
He saw me and we laughed together—
and down he came—and then he hit a rough patch—
put his hands out—one mitten wasn't tucked into the sleeve—
and the palm of his hand got an ice burn.
His grin turned to pure pain and tears sprung flowing freely.
He stopped at my feet.
He looked at me and said: I hurt.
It's an owie—I bent over him, took his small hand in mine, red
and a bit raw now.
He looked at me and said: If you kiss it, it will make it better,
    disarming me utterly. I bent further and kissed his little hand.
And the smile returned—I do it again! And he pulled his mitten
tighter.
He sprang up and took off—
I watched amazed and delighted. In no time at all he was at the
top again—
I know where the mean place is now. Then he shouted again. It
hurts still!
But you can blow some kisses to me—and he held his hand with
his injured palm up—

And I blew kisses. He smiled, and again slid down the hill, stopping at my feet again.
He stood up and smiled at me, cheeks and face glowing with the cold and eyes alight.
He said: I have to go now—can I have one more kiss? Of course!
Weeping I kissed his palm—and off he went. He looked back once, waved his hurting hand—
And was gone. I stood in the cold, holding my heart.

I have a friend who hurts—he's got so many owies I could start kissing him at the first sign of light in the morning and when stars appeared with the dark, I'd still be kissing him (and from a distance). I would blow him kisses, and anywhere they touched, they'd hit an owie (sigh).

One of the Spirit's ancient names is The Kiss of the Mouth of God. I pray the Spirit blows him kisses—always as he waits for the Spirit, his beloved friend, the crucified and risen One to come. He hurts and waits to feel that kiss on his face. Your mouth on his—your breath—to take his breath away. It would be a good way for him to go when it is time, Lord. Until then, I will blow him kisses from you and for you—to ask that you touch his owies—within, bringing him joy and such delight to his face, such wild wonder to his eyes, blunting the pain so he can "do it again"—live with such abandon and trust each day, blessing you. And I, stand in the cold, holding my heart.

Hope

first thing I wrote while/during/after praying—
pen to paper (in pink ink, rose-colored no less!)
at 2:45am...it's a piece on hope—beginning with a
story of God escorting her/Hope on his arm, introducing
her around to his friends—in such dire need of her virtue,
gifts, grace—so long unmet, unnoticed, or appreciated.
She is the oldest daughter, first in line, some wise ones say,
the Spirit's true name, along with wisdom—
esperanza, hope, *spes*, plain named, as crucial as the air we
breathe and as complex and to be held dear as all life itself

"Give an account of your hope"
"Faith is the substance of things hoped for?"

Homecoming for Hope

ONCE UPON A TIME, God gave a party for his friends and took Hope. They entered the party together, she on God's arm. "Come," he said, "and meet some of my friends. They need to know you." (Hope had a tendency to stay on the fringe and didn't mingle much at such gatherings.)

"Come, meet Courage who is sometimes brash, rash, short-lived, arrogant, who rises to the occasion, but doesn't know often how to sustain such response. Here, Hope will help you become enduring grace, steadfast, long-faithfulness (needed for the long haul) without need to see results, without attachment to outcomes."

Next God took her to a rowdy group: many, many folk; all angry. "Come meet the angry ones. They come in many varieties, all hard to live with, and they don't know how to play or really even just to enjoy the life I've given them. They need to know you to grow up with grace. First there are those intent on old hurts, memories of slights and only things done to them; so sad.

"Then come those who blame—loudly, vehemently—anyone, everyone, but take no responsibility for their own actions. They're closely connected to those who see no further than their own pain: insensitive to others', which means nothing to them. They minimal-ize all others—theirs alone being the measuring rod.

"Thirdly are those who are angry because it gives them power, instills fear in others. No one ever knows how they will react, what they will do, erratic, ricocheting wildly out of control, taking plea-sure in how others cringe before them.

"Then there's the next group—those who use their anger to feed depression and self-pity that can become outright despair, befouling all creation, from the weather to disregard of any gratitude or reason to give thanks—unmindful and even disdaining of any goodness that exists—all around them.

"And there are so many who are angry without cause or justification, from simple frustration, unexpected outcomes, being caught off guard, inadvertently exposed, revealed, truth-told—all of which is automatically outright rejected. They refuse conversion. It's easier to continue in one's sin, collusion with evil, even to benefit from others willfully causing distress.

"I know you are strong, Hope—all of these so desperately need your tempering, vision, limitless unselfish urge, expanding consciousness, risking and transforming presence—and most of all your companion Joy, who refuses to be ruled by evil's easy disregard of goodness's more subtle strength and imagination. Come, ease the complaint against the Creator and life itself. You will set them all on the road to liberation and freedom!"

So Hope mingled while God left to check on others, and Hope's eyes wandered—in search of another, kin, soul friend who would not resist so much but would welcome long-range wisdom, even the cross and the burden of bearing another's sorrow and heart's ease.

There was one whom Hope longed to meet. Their eyes, once glanced upon, immediately and always found acceptance, and they moved toward each other, slowly working their way around to the other's presence. God returned and smiled: "Ah, of course, I've waited for you two to meet. Come, Hope, meet my Holy Rage—intolerance of injustice and others' self-righteousness, especially those who profess to believe in me and yet do not resist and stand against evil, abhor violence, or defend others' lives. Long have I sought your bonding, your marriage vows—for of you is born my prophet's anger and compassion, the ones who decry sin and evil in all forms and folk and stand by the truly broken of heart, my beloved poor, and who speaks only my Word. Come together and give birth."

But Hope had one question to ask of the Holy One—*How was I born? Where did I come from?* And God smiled deeply for (or in) answer. "Oh, Hope, my beloved devoted daughter, you were born early, perhaps first born on earth after the fall. You see, humankind chose death rather than life, and so in mercy I kissed Death and you were brought forth, and it was all I could do to recreate it all after such devastation. You are made of Mercy's touch and Death's defeat—an intimacy that so many of my friends still shrink away from....

"Come let me give you away—to all, anyone at all; for without you first, there is no liberation. Even justice is short-lived and short-sighted, let alone Mercy, forgiveness, or ah, Love. You, dear Hope, I fling into the world for everyone to grasp hold of—a lifeline to my presence, sight unseen, mystery that signals transfiguration, the mark of my own Beloved Chosen One's Person and Spirit."

And so Hope leapt down to earth and took up residence—incarnating in all spirit born and bred, still hiding the secret presence of God, deepest need and source of Death's demise and Mercy ascending in the world. Hope springs (not eternally) but with every breath that sustains life. Hope waits for the friends of God to notice her. Once she walked on the arm of God while he introduced her around. Now again, she walks the fringe, looking for those who would befriend her. She hides out among the poor, the broken and bent, the shunned and blamed, the lost and those in pain. Look around; perhaps she's glancing at you even now.

MEGAN
OCTOBER 25, 1997

Third Time Is the Charm

I T WAS THE SECOND leg of a long overseas trip. First a short hop to Denver, now a four-plus-hour flight to Newark. Then it would be a long layover and the flight to Dublin overnight. I settled into my seat—jumbo jet—in the middle section of seats (second from the aisle), though I usually tried for the seat on the end. At least it was a bulkhead and I could stretch my legs and even stand up if I needed for a moment or two.

And my seat mate arrived, the woman with the coveted aisle seat. A black woman, probably in her late fifties or early sixties, with a young child glued to her hip—maybe a little over a year old and on her other side, a large diaper bag with essentials for the long trip and an equally large purse. We smiled. She looked tired already and the baby was squirming and unhappy. I helped her get settled and she went quickly and changed the baby, then came back and we began to resettle for the duration of the flight.

The baby was overtired. We talked. They'd already come from Los Angeles to Denver and now were headed home to Newark, NJ. First time the little one had traveled on a plane, let alone being so far from her home. We took off, and for a while the little one settled and half-slept. I looked at the woman beside me. She was so weary, the strain showed in her face around her eyes and the rest of her body wouldn't relax.

Within an hour the baby was awake. A bottle appeared and we exchanged smiles of relief, after a brief but loud set of cries from the baby. It didn't last long; empty bottle and time to be put to the shoulder and burped. And then more squirming with the little one wanting to get out from being trapped between the seat belt and the woman holding her. Next came crackers, good old Lorna Doones to suck on and chew softly. Again a short respite. We smiled again. It was going to be a long trip.

Then the woman needed to use the toilet, and I held out my arms and the baby was transferred to me. She was a bit taken aback—the woman who was surprised that I'd offered and the baby who was surprised enough not to cry and curious enough to pull at my white hair and finger my face. She returned and settled again. Since the baby seemed OK, she stayed on my lap, and the woman and I began to talk. She wanted to know where I was headed—not to New Jersey, but across the ocean. They were headed home finally, she said, couldn't wait to just settle after a hard trip. I asked polite questions about where in California they'd been and who they had been visiting. She paused, reluctant to answer, so I deflected the questions and asked how old the toddler was—another sad smile this time and she said, "Oh, she's just sixteen months, but she's already gotten old." I didn't respond, though I wondered what she meant. Was the child "an old soul" born, as children sometimes are, with wisdom and a sense of themselves older than most of us ever get with age?

She took a breath and sighed, saying, "You're going to Ireland to talk on families?"

"Yes." I told her I had written a book and there was a big conference there. And then she started to tell me her story.

She began, "It's been a long trip, unexpectedly so. About three or no, four weeks ago, I came out to see my younger sister and to help her during her second round of chemo. I thought I'd stay eight to ten days. She was much weaker than I expected and this little one (still on my lap) is a handful for anyone who's healthy. And my sister started talking almost the first day—about dying. She sensed she wasn't going to make it and didn't have long. I had to face the fact that she was right and then the most important thing was the baby. Who would take care of her? My children, four of them are all grown and I live alone now. I'd been thinking of selling the house and moving in with one of them or maybe into a condo—downsizing, I think they call it. But she asked me straight out to take the baby back with me—what could I say, or do? I'm old enough to be her grandma and more...."

She paused and touched the baby so gently and carefully, bringing a smile to the child's face for the first time I'd seen in nearly two or more hours into the flight.

And she continued. "You see," she said, "the baby wasn't her child. She was born to her next-door neighbor and they were close—a single mom and an older woman (old enough to be her mother) living alone. And then the woman was killed in an accident. At the funeral, my sister found out that the woman, her friend, had asked that my sister take her baby, adopt her, and raise her, which she did. And then my sister got cancer again. Faster this time—

"And she told me she'd made me the child's legal guardian. Would I take her, adopt her and raise her as my own?" There was a long pause. Some tears began and she said, "We buried her four days ago, so now we're going home. I'm taking her to live with me. I'm hoping my children will meet us at the airport and fall in love with her and take her in—that she'll be one of us now."

I was stunned. Overwhelmed. Touched by this woman's care. We played with the baby and I dozed a little, praying for them and their amazing relationship, and mulling over the concept of family—the adopted child of a friend, a single mother, half her age, and then the taking of the child by her sister who had never even met the child or its original mother except through the friendship and love of her sister. How inadequate and false to think of family as mother, father, and child connected by blood or marriage as any norm or indicator of what is a family.

We talked. She dozed. The baby slept being passed back and forth between us. Finally we exchanged names as we started to prepare to land. On the ground in Newark, we embraced with the baby squeezed between us. She was excited—to see which of her children and their families would be waiting to meet them. As we exited the plane and went our separate ways, she asked me for my prayers and I promised I would remember them—always. She smiled again and said, "Maybe the third time is the charm for this little one!" It was a hope, a prayer in itself. And we each went our ways into the grace and wonder of what family might be and how greathearted humans can be. I was so grateful, humbled, and blessed by them that I will not forget. May the third time be the charm for that child. O God, may it be so. Amen.

38138954R00073

Made in the USA
Middletown, DE
06 March 2019

Writing
for IELTS

Anneli Williams

Collins

HarperCollins Publishers
The News Building
1 London Bridge Street
London SE1 9GF

First edition 2011

12

© HarperCollins Publishers 2011

ISBN 978–0–00–742324–8

Collins ® is a registered trademark of HarperCollins Publishers Limited

www.collinselt.com

A catalogue record for this book is available from the British Library

Typeset in India by Aptara

Printed and bound in China by RR Donnelley APS

About the author

Anneli Williams has taught English for academic purposes at university level in the UK for over 15 years, developing extensive experience assessing and preparing candidates for the IELTS examination. Anneli is also the author of *Vocabulary for IELTS* (Collins, 2012).

Author's acknowledgements

The author would like to thank her editors Katerina Mestheneou, Tasia Vassilatou and Howard Middle for their valuable input and Louis Harrison for his advice and support.

Photo credits:

All images are from Shutterstock

Cover: Warren Goldswain; p8: Blaj Gabriel; p16: Paul Cowan, Vlasov Pavel, s74; p24: l i g h t p o e t, vovan, Dustin Dennis, PhotoHouse, Layland Masuda, Mike Flippo, Monkey Business Images; p32: Paul Aniszewski, MartinsL, Anna Omelchenko, Wilm Ihlenfeld, Vladimir Wrangel, Winthrop Brookhouse; p40: Andresr; p48: jean schweitzer, Pressmaster, Stephen Coburn, Andresr, bikeriderlondon; p56: mangostock, Kzenon; p64: Kravtsov Sergey, Zurijeta, Monkey Business Images, GWImages; p72: michaeljung, Halina Yakushevich; p80: Alexey Lysenko, byggarn.se